Frontispiece

Ramstrom's beautiful eight-wheeler and trailer uses a demount system so that, when the container business is quiet, general haulage is carried out using traditional Scandinavian style bodywork.

HIGHWAY HEAVY METAL

The World's Trucks at Work

ARTHUR INGRAM and **MARTIN PHIPPARD**

WITH ADDITIONAL MATERIAL BY
NIELS JANSEN AND PETE SMITH

BLANDFORD PRESS
POOLE · NEW YORK · SYDNEY

First published in the UK 1986 by Blandford Press
Link House, West Street, Poole, Dorset, BH15 1LL

Copyright © 1986 Arthur Ingram and Martin Phippard

Distributed in the United States by
Sterling Publishing Co. Inc.,
2 Park Avenue, New York, NY 10016

Distributed in Australia by
Capricorn Link (Australia) Pty Ltd
PO Box 665, Lane Cove, NSW 2066

Typeset by August Filmsetting, Haydock, St Helens

Printed in Great Britain by
Purnell (Book Production) Ltd Paulton

British Library Cataloguing in Publication Data

Ingram, Arthur
   Highway heavy metal : the world's trucks at work.
   1. Trucking—History
   2. Transit, International—History
   I. Title   II. Phippard, Martin
   388.3'24   HE5613

ISBN 0-7137-1614-2

Contents page

Sisu trucks, built in Finland, not only have extremely advanced
drivelines, but also sport cabs which won several design awards
in Europe in 1984.

CONTENTS

ACKNOWLEDGEMENTS

The Authors would like to acknowledge the following for their help in the preparation of this book:

Arrow Transportation, Vancouver, Canada; Adrian Cypher; DAF Trucks, Holland – Mr G. Werkman; T. Brad Dunkin; Ford Trucks of GB – Mr Gibb Grace; Hungarocamion, Budapest, Hungary; International Trucks (Australia) Pty Ltd; David Lee; Marcus Lester; Leyland Trucks (South Africa); Oshkosh Truck Corporation; Statens-Vakvert, Sweden; VBG Corp., Sweden – Mr Tom Oquist; Volvo Truck Corp. – Mr George Christensson.

Illustrations were kindly provided by:

Mike Beesley: pp. 16, 51, 58, 78, 144, 154 (top left); Bird and Leeney: p. 101; British Road Services: p. 11; D. Child: p. 127; George Christensson: pp. 20 (bottom left and right), 44; Bob Davey: p. 40; Hutchinson Industries: p. 116; Neils Jansen: pp. 66, 67, 68, 69 (top and bottom); 70, 71, 107, 108, 109, 110, 111, 123, 124, 125 (top left), 126, 127, 128, 129, 130; Kenworth, Australia: pp. 28, 62, 73, 146, 151; David Lee: p. 8; Danny Lubjic: p. 79; John Murfet: p. 135; Joseph Peitz: pp. 132, 136; Chris Phippard: p. 143; Jacqueline Phippard: p. 13 (bottom right); Martin Phippard: pp. 10, 17, (top left); 19 (top left and bottom right), 21, 22, 24, 41, 43, 48, 49, 52, 54, 56, 57, 90, 91, 118, 119, 140, 141, 142, 145, 147, 153, 156 (top left), 157; Sisu Trucks: p. 61; Peter Smith Collection: pp. 93, 94 (top left), 96, 97, 102, 103, 104, 105; Sparshatts of Hampshire: p. 134; Steinwinter Lkw und Bus: p. 131; Volvo Trucks, Crissier: p. 15; Dave Wakefield: pp. 9, 12 (bottom left and right), 13 (top left), 15 (bottom right), 23 (top left); White Truck Importers: p. 63;

INTRODUCTION

If events in the field of trucking during the past decade had to be summarised in one word, that word would have to be 'efficiency'.

Since its very earliest days, the road-haulage industry has reacted quickly and positively to changes. Flexibility became its byword but, at the same time, anyone with even a passing acquaintance with road transport will not have failed to notice that it is synonymous with plain, old-fashioned hard work.

The past few years have not changed this situation unrecognisably but have witnessed a period of consolidation in which a great deal of careful and clever 'fine tuning' has taken place. Everyone has improved either his product or his performance and only in this way has the road-transport industry, and the people employed in it, stayed at the forefront of the world's transportation systems.

We have not seen the frequently predicted switch to alternative fuels, such as peanut oil, nor any fundamental changes to established driveline technology, but engine manufacturers have worked hard to squeeze more power from their products while, at the same time, reducing the amounts of fuel consumed. Similarly, truck and component manufacturers have advanced in important areas of weight reduction, aerodynamics and computer-assisted driver-information systems. Meanwhile, body builders have developed materials and techniques which provide truck users with a better vehicle for any given job.

In short, much of the progress made in recent years is hidden beneath the surface and those not directly involved in the real world of trucking might easily overlook even the more significant achievements.

What one cannot fail to have noticed is that this process of consolidation has resulted in a few mortalities and some fine old names have disappeared from the manufacturers' roll. Indeed, a short drive around virtually any of the developed Western countries will quickly confirm the absolute dominance of some marques and, sadly, the almost total absence of others which, until a few years ago, formed an integral part of the industry in that region. It is undeniably sad that names such as Berliet, Saviem, Bussing, Henschel, Dennison, Scot, FBW, Saurer, Hayes and Brockway are just a few of those which have vanished from the truck-building scene and will, in only a few years time, have disappeared from view entirely. The prospect of fewer and fewer manufacturers surviving the cut-throat business of selling their vehicles, and the casualties resulting from this, is most depressing.

Among the more unexpected events of recent years was the unprecedented step of European manufacturers acquiring truck builders in North America. It is doubtless significant that Mercedes, Renault and Volvo, the three largest producers of heavy trucks in the world, should have made almost simultaneous forays into the US market, acquiring all or part of Freightliner, Mack and White respectively. What such moves do highlight is the inescapable fact that we live in a shrinking world. What happens on one side of the globe today can well have considerable effect on a distant, and apparently remote, area tomorrow. The old adage, frequently applied to Western economy, that when one country sneezes, another catches cold, has never been more relevant than today.

The whole make-up of vehicles has changed dramatically over the past few years. True, they still basically consist of a load container carried on pneumatic-tyred wheels, with facilities for it to be started, propelled, turned and stopped at will, but beyond that concept much has been improved.

The outward shape has changed in that many of the 'open spaces' of previous designs have been utilised or filled in by some means. Today's designs treat the vehicle as a whole, with chassis producer, body builder, power-plant and transmission experts all being drawn into the specification at an early stage.

Barreiros-Dodge fortunes changed many times in recent years but although the Spanish manufacturer is now part of the Renault organisation, the original Barreiros design is clearly visible.

The finished truck is a team effort, right down to the producers of trailer couplings, suspension makers, wheel builders and tyre manufacturers.

As competition has increased, so the designs have become more sophisticated, with each producer trying to gain the edge on his competitors. In years gone by, when road conditions and legislation forced trucks to run at comparatively low speeds, the need for a smooth passage of air over the truck was not of paramount importance. All that changed as fuel prices soared, road conditions improved and safety regulations became more onerous.

The 1930s saw a few attempts at streamlining, but these were more for publicity and appearance rather than purely functional reasons. Most post-war designs went as far as having a sloping windscreen or a bow-fronted trailer, but little else. Anyone who has driven a large truck will know of the effect that a strong headwind can have on speed, handling and fuel consumption, especially on the wide open stretches of many long-distance runs.

As vehicle speeds have increased, because of larger or more efficient power outputs from engines, so vehicle builders started taking an interest in air-drag reduction in order to make their products more fuel-efficient. Scale models were the order of the day to start, because the large bulk of a truck, or at least its cab, makes for a large and very expensive wind tunnel but, with more money being channelled into research and development by the larger manufacturers, the required full-scale facilities have materialised. Naturally, the first priority was for the front 'slab' of the truck to be considered and this produced a flurry of interest in cab-top wind deflectors and under-bumper air dams. Next came the vehicle sides, especially that troublesome gap 'twixt tractor and semi, with the result that several manufacturers shaped their cab sides and rear edges to help provide a smoother passage for the air and reduce turbulence. Side fairings have been tried and even the extreme rear end has come in for

some attention in order to smooth the air passage. Side skirts and radiused corners have their followers and even details such as mirror cleanliness have come in for research and action.

The use of a wind tunnel treats the vehicle in isolation and, as we all know, most running occurs with a traffic mix of many types, either passing or meeting. The shaping and encasing has done a lot to increase the efficiency of trucks, as well as to improve their appearance. Even the rounding-off of corners seems to make the truck less aggressive, a useful asset in the continuing battle with the environmentalists. The safety aspect must be improved with the filling in of some of the side voids, such as between front and rear wheels, which are such a danger to cyclists. Even the trend toward close-coupled trailers has a safety spin-off with regard to reducing that gap between truck and trailer which has been accountable for many accidents to cyclists and pedestrian alike.

However desirable the total encasement of trucks may be, there are certain drawbacks with regard to accessibility, cooling, weight and, not least, cost. Some organisations have suggested that engines be

As costs have risen, so transport has become more efficient. Specialised vehicles such as this Belgian glass-carrying trailer are now in service everywhere in Europe.

placed in completely encapsulated containers in order to reduce noise levels but provision must still be made for the power unit to breathe, exhaust and be cooled. Like the rest of the mechanicals, it also needs to be maintained and the removal and replacement of extra panels and soundproofing all has to be paid for at each service interval.

The extra shrouding or panelling used to reduce wind drag on a vehicle can produce problems with regard to cooling of brake drums. This state of affairs has also come to the attention of vehicle-design engineers with regard to the trend of fitting smaller-diameter wheels, for this feature means a direct reduction in the diameter of the brake drums mounted either within, or directly behind, the road wheels and merely increasing the width of the brake drum to compensate for a reduction in diameter is not always possible. This situation could mean a fundamental

change-over to the fitting of inboard brakes away from the road wheels and, again, air would have to be directed there to maintain reasonable working temperatures.

Whatever changes occur in future motor-vehicle technology, we can be certain that development will not stagnate. The trend is towards more efficient machines by way of new techniques in manufacture, helped by the introduction of fresh materials which, for reasons of strength, weight, cost or availability, are better than those of today. It is not merely the truck manufacturers who hold sway in the market. Much development work is undertaken by the component suppliers to the motor trade and the search for

Not content with the original GMC 'Aero Astro', this enterprising owner has added many additional features to his unit in the interest of fuel savings. End result, however, is a remarkably ugly vehicle.

improvement in all manner of units, from engines to exhausts, transmissions to tyres (tires), and brakes to bearings, goes on unceasingly.

There still remains the question of what is the most economic path to take in vehicle building. Some truck manufacturers like to produce as much of the total product 'in house' as they possibly can, while another school of thought supports the policy of offering as wide a variety of options as possible, even if many of the options involve 'buying in' units from specialist producers.

Is the Mercedes-Benz and Volvo policy of manufacturing all the major components necessary for heavy-truck building the key to the undoubted success of both these enterprises in world markets?

History shows that there has been a considerable 'mix' of firms which built their own and others which were virtual 'assemblers'. Even today, some truck builders take great pride in offering a wide range of options to the customer and these options are always on the major units, such as engines, transmissions and axles, and not merely the bolt-on variety, such as couplings, wheels and trim items.

To be too rigid in the policy of 'own build' major items can be disastrous if one misreads the market or, indeed, mismatches the options, so that the truck just does not fit the bill. The motor trade is well known for its dislike of single sourcing of components, whether they be transmissions or tyres. So, to produce the major units 'in house', they must be good.

Another important item is that of local facilities for the supply of spare parts, or indeed the availability of back-up facilities for the servicing and repair of the trucks after they have been hard at work in the field for a while. The most expensive truck in the world is just going nowhere if it is grounded for want of a relatively small and cheap item, such as a brake diaphragm, fuel-line filter or electrical connection, which may even be a bought-in part supplied by a component manufacturer. It is not that local engineers are slow when it comes to the adaptation of other parts in order to keep the vehicle rolling, but it might be hundreds of miles from the nearest repair facility and roadside repairs might be out of the question.

Truck repairers have, over the years, gained for themselves a reputation for the adaptability and flexibility which has kept vehicles on the move for what is

S cenes like this have largely disappeared, thanks to the widespread use of ISO containers.

approaching a century. With the increased sophistication of today's trucks, however, it cannot be long before even the most shrewd and skilful motor engineer is stymied by the sheer complexity and intricacy of what is on the road. The stories of intrepid drivers limping home after having made temporary repairs while miles away from base have taken their place in history. Some vehicles can be brought to a standstill by a flat battery while others have to be carried back home, for they cannot even be towed.

TRUCK TRENDS IN THE '80s

As weights and speeds – and the mileages covered each year – have increased dramatically, so operators have been forced to make decisions about the economic wisdom of keeping older vehicles on the road.

In many cases, the answer has been to invest in new equipment and, as a result, the European truck scene has altered significantly in recent years as stylish new rigs have flooded on to a better, more comprehensive road network. Manufacturers, constantly under pressure to produce lighter, more durable and more cost-effective vehicles have fought desperately to keep ahead of the competition as the race to incorporate the latest technology into the current generation of vehicles has progressed. Today's truck operator is faced with a bewildering array of vehicles, each of which claims (probably with some justification) to offer some particular operational or ergonomic advantage.

The truck scene of the mid-1980s throughout Western Europe is undeniably impressive. Powerful, quiet, comfortable and easy to operate, trucks produced in this decade represent the industry better than ever before, as well as providing their owners with better payloads and improved fuel efficiency. They are also more reliable in service and, perhaps more importantly, are supported by fast, effective breakdown and repair facilities in the event of mech-

Clean, crisp, and efficient. This splendid Austrian OeAF truck-trailer combination with sliding-wall bodywork and a MAN 361 diesel is typical of the 1980s' road-haulage vehicle in Europe.

Unusual visitor to the UK is this Czech Tatra 4 × 4 tractor which features tubular-spine chassis, air-cooled Tatra diesel and twelve-speed gearbox.

Beautiful by any standards is this Dutch 3300 series 8 × 2 DAF unit, seen here coupled to its two-axle trailer. Gross weights in the Netherlands permit 50 tonnes for this rig, but 32.5 tonnes is the maximum in the UK.

anical failure. That the aftercare provided by manufacturers and their distributors has improved, there can be little doubt. In fact, evidence is provided by several who promise that, should parts not be available within a certain time (normally around 48 hours), then they are delivered to the operator free of charge. Such confidence expressed by manufacturers is bound to have a beneficial effect on truck operators.

European truckers have always enjoyed a good road system and even long hauls from one country to another have always been possible without too many complications. As a result, it is possible to stand alongside virtually any major highway and watch a procession of heavy trucks parade past, many having been driven from remote parts of Europe or even Iron-Curtain countries.

Even in the UK, separated from the rest of Europe by a stretch of water, long-haul trucks from France, West Germany, the Netherlands, Belgium, Italy, Spain, Portugal and Switzerland are now commonplace on the motorway and A-class road network. Coastal ports witness the movement of many thousands of foreign commercial vehicles each week

and even the most remote rural village will, at some time, have hosted a foreign vehicle and its driver.

Unlike a few years ago, however, most of the vehicles will be instantly recognisable, regardless of the country of origin, for whereas, even a decade ago, most Western countries produced at least a few makes of their own, the 1980s have witnessed a continuation of the decline in the numbers of truck builders still producing vehicles for sale on the competitive European market. Even trucks from as far afield as Hungary are not startlingly different from the MANs or DAFs on which they were based, although the Raba nameplate may be a little confusing. Similarly, the Fiat and Volvo trucks running from Poland, although quite often unusual 6 × 2 tractors coupled to widespread tandem semi-trailers, are instantly recognisable by anyone with even a passing knowledge of current heavies.

Encouragingly, Spain's sturdy Pegaso and Renault (né Barreiros) trucks still manage to retain an unmistakably foreign appearance which is emphasised by the clutter of warning markers and triangles on the roof and the gaudily-painted tractor units. It is a great shame that the dated but individualistic Barreiros/

Tata trucks, built under licence in India to Mercedes design, form the mainstay of the Indian road-transport scene. Cabs are locally built.

Dodge cab is being replaced by the square lines of the Renault, although on the eight-wheeler this looks extremely impressive.

Equally foreign, but contrasting totally in appearance, are the sombre grey-green East-European vehicles, devoid of frills and driven by resolute, uncommunicative and self-sufficient drivers who never set foot inside a transport Routier or indulge in idle gossip at a friendly watering hole. It is impossible to see the unusual Tatras or Skodas and their colourless, impassive drivers without making comparisons between systems and reflecting on how it is possible that even East-European truck technology has developed so very differently from anything we recognise.

The Greeks, like the Bulgarians, tend to favour Volvo trucks nowadays while the Turks stick to heavy-duty models from Mercedes, Kenworth, Mack and International. These rugged vehicles, easily distinguished by the belly tanks under the trailers, oversized tyres and heavy-duty suspensions, are now a common sight in Europe and even on British roads. That such foreign and 'exotic' vehicles should be regarded as part of the ordinary everyday scene is a reminder of just how our world is shrinking.

Despite the fact that many interesting and exciting marques have disappeared from the roads of the UK and Europe, there is much in the way of compensation for the truck lover. Heavy trucks today are often colourfully decorated, embellished with chrome and stainless steel, or customised to a point where the original vehicle is not identifiable. Semi-trailers are often 'matched' to tractors and catchy names, such as 'brew-liner' and 'chip-liner', are seen on immaculate vehicles hauling beer and potatoes respectively. The

Western Star in Canada built this chunky four-axle truck which grosses 36 tonnes solo and 55 tonnes when used with the pup trailer. The truck-mounted crane assures rapid unloading at the delivery point. Second axle is on air suspension but is not steered.

picture today is one of modern, efficient, purpose-built vehicles going about their job of work with a polished professionalism that is reflected by the people behind the wheel. It is as though everyone in the industry has finally acknowledged the value of the heavy truck and is now keen to present the best possible image to the world at large. The picture is not complete, and far from perfect, but the outline is there and it is simply a matter of time before all the spaces are neatly and colourfully filled in.

Of course, our assumptions about how heavy trucks should look and be operated are based on purely Western ideals and beliefs. Emerging African and eastern countries are less concerned about appearance than functional practicality and, for this reason, basic models, from manufacturers such as Mercedes, Leyland, Mack and, of course, the ubiquitous Volvo and Scania, are found in abundance, operating over terrain that rapidly takes its toll of suspensions and tyres.

In Morocco, little 5-ton Fords and Berliets can be found battling their way over craggy passes in the Atlas Mountains or fording rivers in the lower plains while, in Central Africa, Mercedes and Fiats winch and tow their plodding routes across jungle tracks that would deter even the most sure-footed mountain goat. The emphasis in these cases is on simplicity. Trucks must be both simple to operate and to repair,

Representing the ultimate in terms of specification perhaps is this Swiss Volvo which features a two-thirds width cab, 2.3-m (7½-ft) overall width, extra 2.5-tonne axle and rear-mounted crane. Steel rods are carried on this neat little truck which can gross 19 tonnes under Swiss regulations.

East-European trucks are generally drab and colourless so this Czech Volvo, which sports wheel covers, a Michelin man, vertical exhaust stack and clearance lights is an unusual sight.

so items such as air-assisted clutches are definitely not included in the specification. For this reason, manufacturers build vehicles designed with rugged simplicity in mind. Leyland's Landtrain, a heavy-duty truck devoid of frills and comfort but tough and uncomplicated, is just such a machine and large numbers may be found operating in some of the world's least hospitable regions.

An interesting contradiction in terms of the appearance of trucks in operation concerns Afghanistan, a country torn apart since the Soviet invasion. There, despite the deprivations resulting from what amounts to civil war, countless little Bedford J4Ls are still decorated to a level that, to Western eyes, is simply unbelievable. Cabs are painted in brilliant colours and festooned with brightly polished bits of chrome and aluminium, while virtually every wooden body carries huge paintings of everything from modern jet aircraft, to lions and tigers.

Afghanistan boasts one of the largest trucking companies in operation anywhere, claiming that no less than 900 trucks are used daily. Of these, half are Afghan and half from the USSR and huge convoys travel the one main route across the country into Kabul, bringing in essential supplies from around the world. One commodity which is supplied exclusively from the USSR is precious fuel and this is trucked in daily by dozens of Maz, Kamaz and Ural trucks, which contrast starkly in appearance with their gaily decorated Afghan counterparts. The huge numbers of trucks still in operation there, and the amount of consumer goods still on sale in the markets, indicate that bans on the import of Western goods imposed by the

Soviets are not working effectively and that the road transport system is functioning well in spite of the many problems.

Predictably, India also has a colourful, if outmoded truck scene and the thousands of gaily painted Tata and Ashok-Leylands in operation add still more hues to the myriad of natural shades.

Despite the fact that most vehicles are old, or at least oldfashioned in terms of appearance and engineering, the Indian driver is every bit as proud of his trusty steed as the most meticulous European might be of his Globetrotter. Loading is all done manually, truck-mounted cranes or other such handling aids being completely unknown. But there is no shortage of labour in a country hosting 750 million inhabitants and most trucks operate with a driver and possibly two, or even three, helpers, so adequate manpower is always assured.

The vast majority of trucks in service are four-wheelers, although Ashok-Leyland do still produce the 6 × 4 Hippo for heavier work. Bonneted and forward-control designs are produced by both Tata

V̲ery smart Isuzu six-wheeler and drawbar used in New Zealand on general haulage illustrates how Japanese cab design and overall appearance have improved in recent years.

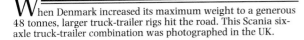

W̲hen Denmark increased its maximum weight to a generous 48 tonnes, larger truck-trailer rigs hit the road. This Scania six-axle truck-trailer combination was photographed in the UK.

H̲aving pioneered the close-coupled drawbar concept, the Dutch went on to improve both payload potential and driver comfort. This smart Volvo combination features a huge roof-mounted sleeper-pod and trailer with close-coupled axles.

and Ashok-Leyland and the emphasis, as expected, is on simplicity rather than sophistication. Indian drivers, are expected to carry out routine servicing and repairs on their beasts of burden, so air-assisted clutches and power steering are not a good idea.

Hindustan is another locally built truck, this marque being based largely on the Bedford but sporting a locally built forward-control cab. Like the Tata and Ashok-Leyland, the Hindustan would not win any prizes in the appearance stakes, but this does not deter its owners from lavishing an inordinate amount of care on it, often to the stage where the truck cab is customised to a point where it is difficult to recognise.

Nowhere on earth is the value of the heavy truck and its driver appreciated to the extent it is in the USA. It is impossible, in fact, to spend even a short time in the country before one becomes aware that the trucking industry is an integral part of everyone's life. There is no namby-pamby anti-truck lobby made up of environmentalists and dyed-in-the-wool railroad enthusiasts who feel that the demise of the rail system is something that never ought to be allowed to happen. The spirit of free enterprise reigns supreme. Whoever provides the best service gets the work. That is the American way and that is the reason trucks and truckers are found in huge numbers from the Atlantic to the Pacific coastlines.

The staggering total of 35 million heavy trucks is the figure put out by the American Trucking Associations in 1985 as representing the number of commercials licensed in the USA in 1984. That is one

truck for every 6.6 persons. No wonder the railway systems are unhappy. And of this vast total, huge numbers of the big rigs are driven by owner-operators, proud, independent truckers, keen to provide a service and to establish their own identity as independent businessmen.

The overwhelming impression of the American owner-operator is of a 'go-getter', someone with the will and motivation to get out there, on the open road and to prove his or her service is the best. It is all part of the North American desire to please and to provide an efficient service. For, in the same way that the American trucker expects quick, courteous, efficient and friendly service from the 'fuel jockey' or coffee-stop waitress, he in turn provides a similar level of service to the shipper.

But all this is not to suggest that the American trucker has had it easy in the 1980s. The recession hit as hard in the USA as in any other part of the globe, but the economy is such that what was a crippling blow to some countries was merely a painful back-hand slap to the USA. Today, the economy and the trucks are again in top gear and carefully specified, beautifully decorated tractor units snarl along the interstate network, delivering the goods to the world's most extravagantly acquisitive nation.

Although there has been a steady increase in the number of appearance-options and convenience-options on long-haul trucks, and although living accommodation areas such as the $40,000 'Liv Lab', with a shower, kitchen and bedroom, are seen in

Steyr trucks are not often seen in the UK, but the latest models are fuel-efficient and comfortable. High-level roof affords extra cab accommodation.

growing numbers, there has also been a trend towards drivelines capable of delivering sensible fuel returns.

Prior to the fuel crisis in 1974, fuel consumption was not really considered of any great importance to the American trucker, who relied heavily on the concept of an endless supply at give-away prices. As a result, trucks were geared to cover the ground quickly, regardless of the expense. Even big diesels, installed in trucks grossing 35 or 36 short tons (31.8 to 32.7 tonnes), were not expected to deliver more than 4 or 5 mpg (Imp.). Items such as air deflectors, and even tubeless radial-ply tyres, had yet to catch on in any big way. The emphasis was on muscle and speed, and big earnings were possible without even considering the price of diesel.

The picture today is very different. Some trucks still run fast, particularly in states that never took kindly in the first place to President Carter's federally-imposed 55-mph speed limit. Montana, for example, turns a blind eye to speeders and Arizona tends to look upon fast trucks with at least a little sympathy. But, overall, speeds have come down and, at the same time, engine manufacturers have done their bit to ensure that trucks go further on the same amount of fuel. The result is a dramatic improvement in overall fuel economy and some truckers now claim that as much as 9 mpg (Imp.) is possible with the right equipment driven in the correct way.

Several different methods of improving fuel returns have been tried, but the most important include de-speeded diesels, and better aerodynamics. In 1979, engines throughout the USA were normally set to run at 2,100 rpm but, today, Caterpillar and Cummins produce big diesels rated for maximum power at a leisurely 1,600 rpm. To compensate for the slower engine speeds, it has been necessary to introduce faster rear-axle ratios and overgear transmissions. The overall philosophy is one of 'gear fast – run slow', an approach which some truckers still find hard to accept

Always a respected name in trucking, Freightliner continue to build trucks which appeal to image-conscious owner-operators. This magnificent conventional incorporates a matched air foil which extends over the sleeper cab.

In Michigan, eight-axle semi-trailers, known as 'centipedes', are used to haul steel coils. Here an immaculate Ford LTL 9000, boasting wire wheels on the tractor and an impressive matching semi-trailer, waits for its 45-tonne load.

but which shows definite improvements in terms of fuel consumption and reduced driveline and brake wear. Major fleets across the USA have almost standardised on engines in the 300-hp to 330-hp range, while owner-operators tend to opt for slightly more power in the 370-hp to 400-hp range. These outputs are a far cry from a few years ago when owner-operators in particular were clamouring for the big 450-hp V8 Cat and Cummins KTA-600s.

Some owner-operators do take the whole idea of productivity very seriously and one such example is Bob de Sliwa, a US trucker who improved the fuel returns on his big CL 9000 Ford cabover from 4.4 to 9.2 mpg (Imp.). The transformation was not simple and changes to the truck involved re-tuning the engine, modifying his own driving technique and, most important of all in his opinion, completely altering the

aerodynamic qualities of his vehicle. This latter stage witnessed the addition of fairings to the front and sides of not only the tractor unit but also the trailer. The CL 9000 already had recessed grab handles and a rounded front end but, by the time De Sliwa had finished with the extra panels, the rig was unrecognisable. Such colossal improvements in fuel returns are not common, but at least the benefits of reduced wind resistance have been proved conclusively. GMC acknowledged this when it introduced a special version of its Astro series dubbed the 'Aero-Astro', a tractor unit which, although essentially a production-line unit, incorporated several stylish, factory-installed fairings designed to ensure that it slipped through the air more easily.

Air-suspension systems on both tractor units and semi-trailers have also caught on in a big way in North America, with many companies now keen to take advantage not only of the vastly improved ride characteristics but also the exactly equalised axle loadings. Less than a decade ago, air suspension was the exclusive preserve of the furniture remover or 'bedbug hauler' but today it is found on trailers hauling any type of load. Even steel haulers use air on their trailers, truckers having learned that, in addition to equal axle loads, mechanical repairs and problems are far fewer.

Belgium recently introduced legislation increasing the maximum gross weight for five-axle tractor-trailers from 38 to 44 tonnes, providing the semi-trailer was equipped with air suspension. At the same time, tri-axle trailers having conventional steel leaf-springs were subjected to a reduction in gross vehicle weight from 26 to 24 tonnes. These moves clearly indicate the value placed on fully-compensating systems, of which air is the best example.

In addition to being used for vehicle suspensions, air is also used to isolate truck cabs from road shocks. The big Ford CL9000, introduced in 1977, was the first model to offer an air-suspended cab among its list of regular, production-line options. Rather unexpectedly, the Yugoslavian truck builder TAM introduced its own air-cab system in 1984, although this has yet to enter full-scale production. TAM produce around 10,000 vehicles per year, the majority for their own domestic market, but with large numbers exported to South Africa.

All TAM trucks are powered by KHD diesels and earlier models were based on Magirus Deutz trucks. The latest range, however, features its own cab and

In Japan, long rigid six-wheelers are used for general haulage. This twin-steer Fuso has the usual forest of mirrors (all of which must be visible through the windscreen), side-under-run guards and a large window in the nearside door.

Japanese van bodies often employ power rams which lift the entire roof and topside of the body skyward for ease of loading and unloading. In Europe, the curtain-sider fulfils the same purpose.

the big T260 T22 three-axle tractor units, powered by Deutz V8 air-cooled engines are modern and clean in appearance. Vehicles in the 3-tonne to 40-tonne gvw range are produced at present.

In the world of trucking, the huge, brightly coloured, multi-axle outfits always seem to hold centre stage, whether at a show or on the road, but this is not a true picture of their importance in the real world of trucks and transport, for their numbers are small by comparison with the swarms of totally unglamorous rigid four-wheelers and six-wheelers, which perform the bulk of the transport and distribution of any country's wealth. For every fancy paint job, there is an army of downright plain trucks going about the down-to-earth job of trucking for profit.

In similar vein, the number of mouth-watering transcontinental rigs is small beer when set against the overall number of load-carrying trucks and the proportion of maximum capacity outfits is far outweighed by the sheer bulk of the total number of load carriers in all classes.

If we put aside all our personal likes for a moment, and take an overall view of the whole field of transport and distribution, it soon becomes evident that a lot of work is done by the plain and unashamed working trucks of the world. While the heavy, long-distance outfits grab most of the limelight, because of appearance, design, power and sheer size, they also attract most of the flak from the anti-truck brigade. The fact that transport is so vital in a civilised country is borne out by the importance attached to its control by political parties.

We all know of the gradual increase in the amount of legislation aimed at curbing the spread of road transport, a lot of it supposedly concerned with safety. In recent years, this great bulk of legislation has been joined by that aimed at lessening the impact of the truck on the environment. In addition, there are the wails of those concerned with the shaking of old buildings and the crumbling of old sewers, and even the wearing of the road surface – all by trucks, of course. No one seems concerned with the fact of essential road transport being delayed by repairs to the roads, more often than not repairs caused and made necessary by local councils, gas boards, electricity

Never big-sellers in the heavy-truck sector in Europe, Ford sell more Class 8 heavy trucks in Canada than Mack or Kenworth. These are popular with owner operators, as well as big fleets, and the LTL 9000 is the premium conventional.

services, water authorities etc, who are hell-bent on using the often all-too-inadequate road space for their wires, pipes, mains or other impedimenta.

Other restrictions are also fiendishly designed to make transportation that much more difficult. Pedestrianisation schemes have become an accepted part of the town-planner's curriculum and every town worth a place on the map strives to have its own. Not that traffic-free zones are unwelcome. The trouble is that so often they are instigated without proper thought for the servicing of the premises covered by the scheme, access if any is at the whim of the local authority and, in some instances, access is granted to certain classes of vehicles all day – except trucks!

Additional curbs on free access to areas is often in the manner of an artificial narrowing of approach roads or the creation of completely false weight restrictions. Another ruse used to increase the cost of truck operation is on the main approach roads at cer-

Representing the latest in Soviet heavy trucks is the Maz 6422 6 × 4 tractor. This particular example features an air spoiler, fancy paintwork and even a V8 Turbo decal. Air-conditioning unit on the cab roof, however, is a dummy module.

tain times of the day. This takes the form of creating bottlenecks and traffic jams by the repositioning of traffic islands and centre road markings in order to force all the cars and trucks into an artificially narrow roadway width, or even into one lane in places where there were previously two. This ploy often forces the traffic to seek an alternative route, much to the annoyance of local residents who are subjected to heavy flows of traffic frantically trying to dodge the long queues which inevitably build up at intersections. The ensuing jams of revving engines at junctions, added to the additional mileage of back-street rat-run routes, all produce a whole cloud of extra anti-environmental fumes which could have been avoided

by improving the road layout instead of introducing traffic mismanagement schemes.

Most of the anti-truck antics are aimed at all trucks, but there are others which are more selective. Width and height restrictions are easy to manage because anyone daring to exercise his freedom via his truck will end up with a bill for damage of one kind or another. The weight restriction is not so easy to control and immediate recognition of whether a truck is 6, 7.5 or 9 tonnes in weight is almost impossible. However, other variations of the prohibitions are encompassed by the bans on trucks by time of day, or even days of the week. The summertime weekend bans on European autoroutes is typical of such moves and the night-time ban of trucks from specific roads is another.

Some years ago, a plan was mooted for central London to be kept free from commuting car drivers by the imposition of an inner-city licence or badge sys-

Greek vehicles are generally gaudily decorated but some are more tastefully finished, as evidenced by this superb Bussing unit. The roomy cab with high level roof and 320-hp made this model a favourite with drivers.

As in all highly industrialised nations, steel plays a vital role and special trailers are built to transport the big strip-steel coils safely from loading point to construction site. This Japanese Fuso is one such example.

tem, together with a hefty payment, of course. This did not materialise but recently a similar plan to ban – yes, you've guessed it – trucks from a huge area of London has made front-page news and been the matter of heated debate from all sides.

But where there is business to be done in this world, there are luckily still those irrepressible entrepreneurs who bounce back in the face of all the opposition and devise ways to get round the restrictions imposed by those who would like to see transport return to the days of wheelbarrows.

With all the problems facing the congested and restricted town areas, many of the larger retail stores are turning their backs on the accepted locations and opening up larger premises on new sites situated just outside the towns for which they cater. This fresh facility allows a one-floor approach, with ample room for the delivery, storage, display and sale of the produce and, more importantly, adequate access for the customers and private parking areas. As one can guess, this system does not please everyone and soon the local authorities will be wailing that these massive out-of-town shopping areas are taking the life out of the town centres. Yes, the very town centres which helped drive out the business by virtue of their high

Unusual by any standards are the GMC Astro tractors operated by French refrigerated haulier, Transnoeuxois. Units feature cab spoilers which also afford increased internal roof level for extra crew-living area.

rates, poor access and restrictions on would-be customers.

Another sphere of anti-truck work is the way in which the truck driver himself suffers, not only from the various bans and restrictions mentioned earlier, but from the non-provision of facilities. With the building of exclusive motor roads, the old roads by-passed by the new routes have fallen into decay and, with them, the much-used rest and refreshment locations. The new motorways have their modern cafés and restaurants, but with a noticeable bias towards the car-driving public, holiday traveller and coach passenger. In some countries, even the parking areas are carefully laid out, with trucks being positioned as far from the shops and toilets as possible.

Invariably, the truck driver finds himself in a built-up area at the end of his working day and then his troubles can really begin. Usually there are local bans on the overnight parking of trucks in the town so he has to head off for the appointed truck park – if there is such a thing. Having found the place, it invariably turns out to be as welcoming as the county jail and often just as inaccessible. But of course there are a few that strive to make one's stay as pleasant as possible, with all the creature comforts that one could expect for the charge made. All too often though, these parking places have no facilities and, in addition, no transport to the more friendly and livelier places usually to be in town. The parking lot is usually located either behind the gasworks or on a disused railway siding or the like.

If the truck has a day cab then the search for a bed for the night can be just as depressing. In industrial areas, overnight accommodation is very limited and, in holiday areas, most guest-houses book only by the week, especially during the season. Coupled to all this is the absurdly low rates that are often paid to drivers for their overnight stay away from home. The way in which some companies have wildly differing meals and accommodation allowances for truck drivers *vis-a-vis* representatives is a classic case of prejudice. In addition, the truck driver is sorely restricted by way of the tachograph during the day and by having no per-

Used primarily to move containers inside the Netherlands, this DAF eight-wheeler and tri-axle trailer represents a combination designed to combat the problem of overweight containers.

sonal transport in the evening with which to reach a possibly better place to stay.

All these factors go toward the trend among drivers to get back home at almost any cost, either by hitching a lift or by turning their backs on the meagre facilities on offer and enduring a cramped night within the confines of the cab, pocketing any allowances for the sheer inconvenience of it all.

On the other side of the coin is the absolute independence that can come from a trucking life, for it is undoubtedly one of the world's easily attainable means of working freedom, especially in some of the more remote parts of the globe. Much has been written concerning the glamorous side of the job and the parallel with the old-style US cowboys but, in other parts of the world, the term 'cowboy' has become synonymous with that fringe of the transport industry where everything is done on a shoe-string, with little regard for the safety and well-being of others. The fact

that the truck-driver's life can be attractive to some is indisputable, for it can offer a tremendous amount of freedom and the chance to develop one's state of self reliance and individuality. Some older men bemoan the fact that the job has changed out of all recognition in the past few decades, but then so have most other things, not least of all the trucks themselves. Older truckers can often be heard relating stories of days gone by when, if you were stranded by a breakdown, there was always another who would stop to help whereas today, they say, everyone is in a mad rush to get on and you are left at the roadside. This is probably true for a number of reasons. With the high cost of transport and the competitiveness of the business, any delay is to be avoided. In addition to this, the 'tacho' is ticking away the shrinking working day and an hour's delay could mean a missed load. Also, as trucks get more reliable and breakdowns fewer, so the driver gets less involved in the mechanics of what he handles as well as which, the vehicles themselves get more complicated as the years roll by. Still further is the fact that, in highly commercialised areas, the repair centres are never far away. If you changed all that for a less inhabited and less hospitable area, you

The bonneted Hino range of vehicles is particularly well suited to the rigours of on/off highway construction work. Hard at work on a major bridge-building project are two 6 × 4s.

can be sure that truck drivers still stop to help one another.

It is unfortunate that, in the eyes of the general public, our truck driver does not rate very highly. Over the years, the job has attracted some kind of stigma as being run-of-the-mill and dirty, the sort of job that one will take when nothing better is available. Luckily this state of affairs is gradually being eroded and not before time. One way that has helped the industry and, at the same time, assisted in making the job more attractive, has been a raising of the skill necessary to obtain a licence. Higher standards of driving through better training have helped put the job on a higher plane. Other improvements have come about through better wages and conditions, more acceptable hours and the provision of clothing and other benefits. The improvements in body and cab design have helped the driver maintain a cleaner image and no one will mourn the day that those acres of sheets and miles of soggy rope disappear from a truck driver's equipment.

Various styles of truck-driving competitions,

The humble four-wheel truck carries its share of commodities around the world. Note the ever-popular curtain-sided body.

Of greater public-relations value must be the various contests of driving skill carried out under strictly controlled conditions. Unfortunately, these events lack the lustre and excitement of the truck races and are usually followed closely only by family and friends of the participants, who already appreciate the importance of truck drivers to the national economy. A greater public awareness of trucks and the importance of the trucking industry will probably follow instances of combined events which allow the public to witness the calm and concentration of the entrants in the safe driving competitions, followed by a few laps of the decorated and jostling heavies as they battle to see who can get round a circuit the fastest and stay upright!

Returning to the everyday world of working trucks, we find that they obtain different reactions from Joe Public according to the country of operation. Some countries seem to have a much more liberal approach than others, for they appear to accept the truck for what it is, a means of bringing in the goods and services that are required by the community, as well as providing a certain level of employment and wealth. Unfortunately, others have a differing view probably where other forms of transport abound, especially if they have state connections.

Luckily for us, the world is never without its daily supplies of food and drink and other consumables which inevitably are brought, sometimes literally, to our door by the humble truck and its driver. It is the local delivery truck which comes closest to the people in the streets and it is the one which should best project the image of clean, safe and efficient transport. Many of our retail organisations are at last realising its importance.

A phenomenon of the past decade or so has been the realisation by some of the large retail organisations of the power they can exert over their suppliers. Not many years ago, it was the manufacturer who would detail the criteria to be met regarding deliveries to customers' premises. It was often a case of: 'You will get your load on a Monday because that is the day our truck comes to your area', or words to that effect.

With the tremendous changes which have taken place in the field of retailing over the past 20 years,

F airings around the side of the cab, as well as those above, give this impressive SAR Australian Kenworth a strange appearance.

rodeos, shows and rallies have brought trucks and their drivers into closer contact with the general public and anything which displays its skills gains greater acceptance from all concerned. One recent phenomenon of the truck world which really seems to have caught the imagination of a great section of the public is that of truck racing. This has gained a great following in a relatively short space of time, although its value to the trucking industry generally is a matter of intense debate. Some companies have seized upon it to promote their wares, whether trucks, tyres or tachographs, while others have steered very clear of it and a few have actually said that they cannot support it in any way, nor understand how it can help the image of the trucking industry.

Some truck and component manufacturers themselves carry out high-speed testing for various reasons, but this has no competitive element to it, being purely for engineering and evaluation purposes and part of regular research and development programmes.

Engaged on international removals, this DAF 2100 shows some of the latest trends in the bid to stay competitive. Note the roof-top sleeper which doubles as a wind deflector, the under-bumper air dam, side-panelling and sculptured cab sides, all aimed at fuel efficiency.

and the greater purchasing power in the hands of the public, together with fierce competition in the food, drink and clothing trades, the emphasis has swung in favour of the giant retail chains. Anxious to maintain their position and to expand if at all possible, the multiples now demand deliveries to suit their merchandising plans. With the high cost of warehousing and transhipment, the arrangement is to deliver a full load to one address if possible, for every time the bulk load is broken down into smaller units, the cost soars. Failing this 'one truck, one drop' system, the retailer may demand that several different lines for one consignment are pre-assembled by the transport operator and then delivered at a predetermined time. There are a number of specialist carriers who do nothing else but supply a service dedicated to large retail chains.

This arrangement also extends to some of the smaller retailers who order a wide range of merchandise from a specialist wholesaler who then arranges deliveries on one vehicle. Some of these smaller outlets also band together in a form of purchasing co-operative in order to secure better terms and feel more able to use a bit of 'muscle' to coerce the supplier to bend to their wishes.

There are varying degrees of specialisation among the fleets dedicated to carrying for particular manu-

Kraz six-wheel dump-trucks have established a reputation for reliability and durability in the many Eastern bloc countries in which they are used. These examples are seen climbing out of a village in Yugoslavia.

facturers or wholesalers or retail outlets. For very many years, the majority of producers used their own transport, and some set up wholly-owned subsidiary companies purely for the carrying side of the operation. This latter operational style does give the parent company some degree of extra control by way of making the subsidiary stand up by its own financial strength and efficiency, for it may have to quote in direct competition with an independent carrier for the business.

Other variations include companies which keep a

minimum fleet to handle the low demand period, hiring for the peaks. Some hand the whole operation over to a haulier who supplies the vehicles painted in the appropriate livery, supplies the drivers, arranges the reliefs, covers the maintenance and looks after all aspects of the fleet. Others may have no transport operation at all and rely purely on a professional haulier who carries whatever is offered. Variations on this include trucks in the hauliers' colours, vehicles liveried in the name of the customer, or even plain vehicles for security or other reasons.

Some large organisations will even have dedicated fleets supplied by more than one haulier, with dry goods being handled by one contractor while temperature-controlled traffic is handled by another specialist.

Special low-height body for the soft-drinks trade constructed by Bonallack and mounted on an adapted Leyland Freighter with drop frame from back of cab to rear axle.

For many years, those concerned with the delivery service have realised the importance of maintaining a safe, convenient and economic system which did not rely on the sheer strength and fortitude of its drivers. This has meant taking a long and calculating look at the whole field of physical distribution from end of production line to the store shelf. Not least in importance has been providing an efficient vehicle with a sensible level of load accessibility for the driver making the deliveries, and this means bringing most of the load within easy grasp by means of a low floor.

One area of operation where a low-loading height is essential is that of drink distribution, where much of the load is still moved by hand. Historically, the drink trade centred around beer in large casks – originally wooden, but later metal. Although extremely heavy, the shape of the casks did make handling easier than one would expect. Then two things happened in the beer trade: the cask-beer customers were switched on to bulk tanks in the cellars and the High Street market went further into bottles and cans. There was also a

movement away from the traditional off-licences and into the supermarkets for the carry-home trade. The bulk-tank aspect of delivery meant an easing of problems, while the tremendous increase in smaller packages of beer generated a whole new area of handling and storage problems.

As the main ingredient of beer is water, it is naturally a heavy commodity. The packaging in glass bottles or thin metal cans, and now even plastic bottles, means that adequate protection is necessary during transit and handling, and the delivery point is often some distance from the delivery truck and more often than not at a different level. All these factors have a bearing on the distribution system and the aim has been to make the handling as easy and safe as possible by using low-loading trucks.

Old methods of loading the vehicles included hand stacking off a loading bank or from a conveyor; later on fork trucks were used, with loading taking place either from the rear at bank level or from ground level over the side. So loading was no great problem; it was at the delivery end that the going got tough, when usually the only aid to handling was a plank down which to slide the boxes or a sack-truck to wheel them away. A minimum of two men was required and, more often, three men were the order of the day. With

F̲or many years, the Motor Panels company has produced good cab designs for use by various truck-chassis builders. This is their Hemi-Tech design which embodies a fold-down roof-mounted sleeper area.

labour costs on the climb, attention naturally turned to making life easier for the crew in the vain hope that manning levels could be reduced. One of the main gripes was vehicle deck height and load security; a high floor means plenty of climbing up and down at

every drop and lorry sheets meant continually having to sheet and unsheet as the day wore on.

Any reduction in load height could only be achieved by the paring down of the actual thickness of the vehicle floor and its supporting frame attached to the chassis. Beyond that, it was a case of reducing wheel diameter and tyre size. To do this often meant reducing the load capacity, because carrying capacity is related to tyre and wheel sizes as these carry the weight. Some designs allowed the tyres and wheels to remain constant, merely lowering the floor around the wheel area and providing protruding wheelboxes with flat tops to carry some of the load. Others did reduce wheel and tyre sizes and then added another axle to offset any reduction in vehicle capacity. First attempts used single-drive rear bogies, with the resulting problems of lack of traction on undulating ground, such as car park entrances. The next attempt was to reduce wheels and tyres yet further and add another axle. After this, the twin-steering layout was tried, thus still providing three axles yet obviating the problems of single-drive bogies. Still another idea was to produce miniature low-loading artics which had the benefit of an ultra-low loading floor but the drawback of being rather overlength for the loads carried.

A fresh approach to the problem was the central-spine chassis which remained at the original chassis height but with the load deck hung much lower. By this method, the wheels and tyres are of the normal truck size so two axles are ample but only the space between the front and rear wheels is available at the low height, the wheelboxes still being at the higher level. The central-spine chassis also has the drawback of precluding the use of a flat floor but this is of minor importance on local delivery work, where often the load is arranged 'sided' for driver convenience.

A much more fundamentally different, and indeed spectacular, answer to the problem is that introduced by Titan in collaboration with Coca-Cola in West Germany. This revolutionary design takes a fresh approach by virtually hanging the body by its roof from the overhead chassis frame, which forms a high arch and connects the cab at the front with the power unit and drive wheels at the rear.

LOOKING AT LAW-MAKING

Legislation is not a subject likely to elicit anything more than a stifled yawn from most truck buffs and indeed the word itself is sufficiently boring to send most into a state of alertness equalled only by the Sleeping Beauty. But more than anything else it is the rules and regulations imposed by governments which affect the size, shape and overall appearance of any commercial vehicle.

Even to the untutored eye, the differences between say, the trucks used in Italy and those used in North America are glaringly obvious. And who can have failed to notice the vast number of changes to the British truck scene which resulted from the 1983 ruling which allowed 38 tonnes on five or more axles?

All these differences and changes are the direct result of legislation and, because both central and local law-makers jealously guard their rights to effect new rulings, possibilities of harmonisation are remote. Trucks will continue to retain an appearance which identifies them immediately with one country, or possibly even one specific state or region within that country.

This individuality is much appreciated by the truck lover and it is fascinating to watch the true expert extracting detailed information about a vehicle from a photograph simply by using his powers of deduction. In much the same way as Sir Arthur Conan-Doyle's famous detective, Sherlock Holmes, observed and reasoned in order to collect his 'clues', the serious student of road transport uses his knowledge to identify not crooks but commercial vehicles. Apparently obscure facts, such as a truck's load, origin, destination, gross weight, engine size, body builder etc can sometimes be determined from a photograph. In one instance, an astute observer deduced that a particular photograph

had been taken on a Monday, his reasoning being that 'the week's washing on the clothes-line' in the background suggested that it could indeed have been taken on the traditional washday. But this level of expertise extends beyond the study of transport!

Most visible among the effects of legislation are the dimensions of a vehicle, the number and spacing of axles and its overall configuration, i.e. whether it is a truck, truck-trailer, artic, double and so on. But much legislation is hidden away beneath the skin of today's truck and this includes the size of engines, which are governed by power-to-weight requirements, supplementary braking devices, or emission controls affecting smoke and noise.

It goes without saying that it is in the countries of the developed Western world that legislation has had its greatest effect and, from this, it may be reasoned that, in countries where there is little or no law controlling truck operation, there is more variety in the types and configurations of vehicles. In fact, the opposite is true for, where there is legislation which controls the standards to which trucks must be built, the ingenuity of engineers and operators often combines to design and build vehicles capable of doing a job while, at the same time, satisfying the exacting requirements of the government's transport department.

As a direct result of this inventiveness, some extremely interesting vehicles have been produced in many different countries. One of the best examples is Switzerland, whose obsession with efficiency has resulted in highly specialised trucks and trailers. In fact, most of Europe's leading manufacturers build at least some models exclusively for the Swiss market, an exercise which is really cost-effective for only a few.

An overall width limit of 2.3 m ($7\frac{1}{2}$ ft) and a 10-hp-per-tonne power requirement are the two factors which have most affected the trucks used in Switzerland. No less than 65% of all Swiss roads carry a 2.3-m width limit (the rest of the world has a limit of either 2.5 or 2.6 m, i.e. 8 ft $2\frac{1}{2}$ in or 8 ft 6 in) and, in order for truckers to provide a service anywhere within their country, there is no choice but to buy and operate a vehicle built to conform to this odd requirement.

For many years, the industrious Swiss produced their own trucks, with Saurer-Berna and FBW all building trucks renowned for their safety, comfort and total reliability. In fact, these marques were sold with the assurance that a 20-year life expectancy was the norm. But they were expensive to produce and, little by little, their domination of the market was eroded by Mercedes, Volvo, Scania and others, all of whom were keen to grab a chunk of the lucrative Swiss market.

In the early stages, these imported models were little different from those offered elsewhere in Europe and their use was confined mainly to long-haul operations outside of Switzerland. But it was quickly perceived that, in order to gain a really good foot-hold, it was necessary to offer a 2.3-m ($7\frac{1}{2}$ ft) wide vehicle and soon the search was on to discover the best method of achieving this.

Perhaps the best-known solution is that provided by Volvo, whose CH230 models use the 'British' F7-style cab, slimmed down to 2.3 m ($7\frac{1}{2}$ ft) in width by fitting the front wings flush to the side panels. However, the F7 driveline is not in keeping with the requirements of the Swiss and so the much beefier F12 driveline is installed beneath the raised F7 cab. This provides the hp-per-tonne requirement and satisfies all the legalities. The net result is that, today, Volvo is the second largest supplier of trucks over 16 tonnes to the Swiss market, first place of course going to Mercedes, whose acquisition, in 1983, of Saurer and FBW immediately assured them of access to customers of the two Swiss companies. Unfortunately for Mercedes, however, some Swiss operators strongly resented the fact that the ubiquitous three-pointed star had not only taken over, but had swallowed up without trace their respected and much loved indigenous products. Resistance to the overtures of Mercedes by such people has been strong and it seems likely that, almost for spite, some long-term Saurer and FBW users will buy Volvo, Scania or even MAN as a token of their displeasure.

Heading west across Europe and out across the Atlantic Ocean, we find that, in the USA, legislation controlling truck sizes and weights is the responsibility of each individual state's transportation department. The result of this bizarre situation is, as everyone knows, a mishmash of contradictory laws apparently designed with the express purpose of preventing coast-to-coast operation.

Incredibly enough, this problem – which was hardly in the best interests of efficiency – was allowed to continue from 1935 to 1982, at which time a federal law was introduced which decreed that, on major interstate routes, single trailers up to a maximum of 48 ft (14.6 m) in length could be hauled, regardless of the overall length of the combination. Known as The Surface Transportation Assistance Act, this legislation was to have a profound effect on the appearance of American eighteen-wheelers because several states in the union were blatantly 'anti-truck' and, prior to 1982, rigidly enforced length limits of 55 ft (16.8 m) overall. With the industry 'standard' 42 or 45 ft (12.8 or 13.7 m) semi-trailers, this effectively ruled out conventional tractors altogether and made things difficult even for the operators of long-wheelbase 'western-style' cabovers.

The solution (and there generally is one although it invariably involves additional cost) was for coast-to-coast truckers, who are usually independents, to equip their tractors with air-slide fifth wheels, controlled from the cab, and their semi-trailers with sliding bogies which could be juggled to and fro along the underside. Another major problem involved the location of fridge units on semi-trailers, since the snug fit required between the rear of the cab and the front of the semi precluded the use of nose-mounted fridges. Here the answer was to mount the fridge underneath the trailer, a location which was obviously far from ideal for reasons of air flow and susceptibility to damage from debris left on the highway.

The long-awaited increase of gross weights in the UK culminated with the 38-tonne limit in 1983, which has seen a profusion of five-axle outfits and quite a number of six-axle combinations taking advantage of the new limit.

It was not only the independents who employed these gadgets either. Some of the major trucking companies used their own ingenuity to beat the vagaries of state jurisdictions and Consolidated Freightways (CF) went so far as to design and eventually operate a rig known as a 'truck-tainer', which posed as a rigid-and-drawbar on the east coast, but which mysteriously stretched to a doubles combination once it reached the safety of the areas where doubles were legal. These outfits, which had more moving parts than a contortionist, were criticised at the time by *Overdrive* magazine (the voice of the independent trucker in the USA) on the grounds that they were unsafe. It is more likely, however, that the technology employed in them was expensive and therefore not available to the independent and that the people at *Overdrive* considered CF to have an unfair operating advantage.

Today, owner-operators in their outrageously lengthy conventional tractors can truck on across the entire country, hauling a trailer up to 48 ft (14.6 m) and waving two fingers in the air, provided of course that they don't stray from the interstate network. It was federal law which imposed the unpopular 'double nickel' 55-mph (88-km/h) speed limit in the interests of fuel economy and now it is the same federal ruling that has allowed this unprecedented freedom of movement from one side of the country to the other. One wonders, however, if USA independents have ever heard the 'swings and roundabouts' theory.

Examples of governments introducing legislation which benefits truck operators without also imposing a bewildering number of conditions are rare, but some governments do at least appear to understand, and possibly even appreciate, the importance of a controlled but not constricted road-transport industry. For instance, whereas British operators were given the opportunity to run five-axle artics (tractor-trailer combinations) at the gross weight of 38 tonnes in May 1983, this 'opportunity' was so bedevilled with conditions that many decided the extra costs and problems involved made the exercise unworkable. It was a classic case of an anti-truck government wanting to be perceived by Europe to be in step, while at the same time doing its best to maintain its protectionist policies on behalf of the railways and satisfy the growing numbers of environmentalist groups. Scant attention was paid to the rising costs brought about as a result of this decision.

On the other hand, some governments really are in touch with transport costs and appreciate the role of the heavy truck in today's consumer society, which requires that goods are not only available, but are available instantly.

When Denmark increased its maximum gross weights from 44 to 48 tonnes at the start of 1984, the Danish Department of Road Safety even agreed to a new 'interpretation' of the legislation which would have otherwise made 6 × 2 tractor units and rigid

trucks incapable of conforming. As these vehicles make up almost 90% of the real heavies, it was obviously nothing short of stupidity to restrict their use, so the government adopted a realistically flexible approach and modified the ruling accordingly. More evidence of their willingness to work with, rather than against, their truckers, was seen in the fact that the introduction of the new weight limits was timed to conform with the wishes of the various Danish road-transport associations. In this case, a period of 6 years was allowed to pass between the time of the increase to 44 tonnes in 1978 and the most recent increase, thereby allowing operators sufficient time to write down the new equipment purchased in 1978. That such co-operation should appear remarkable rather than normal indicates clearly that most of the world's truck operators expect that their governments will be obstructive.

There are those governments, however, whose legislation appears nothing short of sinister. In South Africa, for instance, you can have any sort of diesel in your truck provided that it is an Atlantis!

Atlantis Diesels are in fact licensed manufacturers of Mercedes and Perkins diesel engines. The company has the exclusive manufacturing rights and the adoption of this odd system is supposedly done in the interests of South Africa's economy by guaranteeing local content. All engines are covered, the Perkins 6.354 in various guises covering the lower end of the weight scale and Mercedes having the lion's share with their OM352 and OM400 series and the really powerful OM422 and OM423 V8s and V10s.

What this ruling means in practice is that not only do manufacturers hoping to do business in South Africa face a bewildering array of vehicle standards, but every truck they sell must be designed to accept a Perkins or Mercedes power plant. This has caused much heartache among all truck builders except, of course, Mercedes, who have merely had to change their engine and transmission sourcing from West Germany to South Africa. Gearboxes are also produced locally under licence from another German manufacturer, ZF, but although they enjoy tariff protection, fitment is not mandatory, as is the case with engines.

Most countries attempt some level of protectionism, though few carry the exercise as far as South Africa does. Australia insists on a high level of locally-sourced materials, yet its government never awarded a contract to either of its two indigenous truck builders, RFW and Leader, which both companies claim was at least partly responsible for their failure in the early 1980s. Other governments, such as that of the USSR, although wishing to remain independent of the West, rely heavily on its technology or even the importation of complete vehicles. This situation represents the opposite face of protectionism.

California, home for the rich and famous, noted for its casual, laid-back life style and birthplace of the hippie movement in the 1960s, was also forward-thinking enough in 1967 to pass legislation allowing the use of triples on specified highways. Not to be outdone, northerly neighbour Oregon introduced a similar ruling a few months later, but with one important condition. Oregon is a state that receives more than its fair share of rainfall and its highways department stipulated that, when the roads were wet, the triples parked up. It was not a popular decision among truck men but at least triples trucked on unhindered for much of the year and other motorists felt less inclined to lobby for a reduction in the size of vehicles in their state if they were not swamped with spray from triple-trailer combinations. The logic is obvious. This legislation, like much other, was designed not so much in the interests of safety as for the purpose of keeping the voters happy.

Petitions by interested parties, such as the Oregon Trucking Association, to the Highway Division pointed out the transparent thinking behind the legislation and asked for proof that triples were less safe in wet weather than in dry. But no-one was listening. Joe Public, the voter, saw triples pull off to the side of the highway when it started to rain and was convinced that this was in his interest. Government knows best.

Meanwhile tests conducted by the Western Highway Institute to investigate spray-suppression systems were not going well. Most ideas involved encapsulating the entire rig, which meant that everything beneath the skirt overheated in warm weather and that all the extra material had to be removed for maintenance. Even changing a tyre by the roadside would have been a day's work. But individual experimentation was more successful and Walter Reddaway, an Oregon-based trucker, worked out for himself that, if you fitted the plastic matting known as Astro-Turf to the sides and wings of a vehicle, the spray from the wheels was considerably reduced.

It was not until 1976, however, that Reddaway convinced Monsanto Chemicals that his idea was marketable and that truckers in Oregon could probably benefit from it by being able to run their triples in the rain. More representation was made to the Highways Division, more experiments took place and, finally, in 1980, some operators were given special authority to run their triples in any weather, provided all axles were equipped with Monsanto's 'Spray Guard' system. It was an important day for all concerned.

Today triples are operating throughout the year in Oregon and no-one even notices. The typical 100 Imperial gallons-per-minute (454 l) displaced by a truck tyre in heavy rain (at speeds of 55 mph/ 88 km/h) can total 2,600 Imperial gallons-per-minute (11,800 l) if applied to a triple-trailer combination and even this amount is satisfactorily contained by the various suppression systems used. Cab-mounted air foils and other aerodynamic aids reduce the spray hazard still further by improving the profile of the rig. In the UK today, a great deal of doubt still lingers as to the effectiveness of spray-suppression devices, but in Oregon the government and the private motorists are convinced, and there's no way the truckers are about to start an argument!

BOXING CLEVER

The International Standards Organisation (ISO) container as we know it today came about because of a need to handle a substantial amount of cargo in a single, enclosed, secure and easily transferable manner between the three main forms of surface transport: road, rail and sea.

Who knows when the first carpenter was asked to construct a box large enough to contain all someone's belongings; it was then but a simple step to fit some lifting hooks in order to make the whole thing easier to handle with slings or some similar device.

Containers of varying sizes have long been in use by the railways of many advanced countries for easier handling of various commodities in bulk, or at least in large numbers. Even in the days of horse transport, there were 'lift vans' in use by contractors engaged in overseas trade and these early types of container helped speed up the transfer of goods traffic from road to rail to ship. The railways probably did most to standardise on certain sizes of container which were common to both their rail and road rolling stock. They experimented with many types of container for the multitude of differing traffics they handled in the days before road transport came into its own. There were flat, open, covered and insulated types to expedite the traffic to its markets. Containers also helped eliminate transhipment and terminal delays.

The ISO container was necessary in order to speed the flow of goods on a worldwide basis, such is today's volume of international traffic, and it was also high time that some form of standardisation was instituted in order to cut manufacturing costs and ensure complete interchangeability the world over. Even today, regional variations apply to containers which, for parochial reasons, are made to differing dimensions but, getting back to the main point, the ISO boxes are primarily designed to help the flow of international traffic.

In the 1950s, when the ISO container project first got underway, it was difficult to estimate the tremendous impact that the 'boxes' would have on the transport structure in the years ahead. Shipping lines, freight forwarders, railroads, hauliers, dock owners, in fact almost everyone connected with freight handling on an international, and later national, scale, began to get involved with the new transport mode and realise its vast potential. The resultant growth was phenomenal. Very soon, containers were being used for the most unlikely loads, such as bulk grain, scrap metal and household rubbish, in addition to the more usual ones of foodstuffs, clothing, parcels and carpets.

The range of designs soon expanded from the original boxes to include open-topped ones for top-loading or overheight cargo, space-framed tankers, flats with fold-down ends for easy stacking, types with a rear hatch for end tipping or with doors at both ends for ease of loading, sheet-sided models for side access and even a style with folding doors all along one side for maximum accessibility.

Naturally, life in the container world is not all plain sailing and there have been problems along the way. Means of securing containers to the carrying vehicle was one of the early problem areas, especially after a few spectacular accidents involving ones which were secured by just rope or chains. The approved system is by means of cast steel 'twist locks' which, in the case of a flat trailer, are captive within the trailer floor and flush with its surface until raised and locked in the 'up' position. After the container has been lowered onto them, the twist locks are rotated inside the bottom four of the eight corner castings and so secure it to the trailer. The ISO design includes substantial corner posts which are capable of taking the weight of the loaded container, hence the widespread use of skeletal trailers with no floor, which are specifically produced for container work. The provision of securing eyes in the top corners of the containers is to allow

the easy stacking of containers in both full and empty states, for the weight is taken through the corner pillars and not the main shell of the container.

Another spin-off from the use of ISO boxes has been the setting up of inland container depots at a distance from the actual port of entry. This has enabled shippers to by-pass docks which had a history of labour problems. Similarly, new docks have come into prominence purely as container ports, these being specifically designed to turn round container-carrying vessels at a fast pace. Massive investments have been made at these ports in order to expedite the handling of freight boxes, with huge areas of clearly marked storage space for the systematic temporary storage of thousands of ISO containers. Special cranes and other lifting tackle have come into use, together with sophisticated monitoring systems in order to maintain close control of the tremendous flow of traffic in and out of the premises.

In certain countries with the strict legislation on vehicle gross weights, the use of containers has brought it s own problems. Often the container is load-

Designed specifically to haul 'trains' of containers around the busy docks at Rotterdam, this ballasted DAF 3300 is pictured with no less than eight 20-ft (6-m) ISO containers in tow. Dutch-built FTF tractors also perform this task.

ed by people with little regard for its ultimate movement or its legality with regard to weight. Not only is there the problem of excessive gross weight but, in certain cases, a large proportion of the weight can be at one end without the overall gross being exceeded. This imbalance may not be apparent to anyone merely check-weighing the vehicle as a whole as it leaves the dock – but, in reality, an offence is possible should the unfortunate driver be ordered to take the vehicle over a purpose-built weigh-scale and it is found that one axle is overloaded.

Another problem with containers is that of damage suffered whilst in transit, for most spend long periods away from base and in the hands of various transporters. This aspect of container use has given rise to the establishment of specialist container-repairers.

Although road haulage in Africa is generally regarded as being very basic, countries such as Zimbabwe in fact boast a fairly sophisticated industry. Here a locally-built AVM 6 × 4 hauls two 30-ft (9.1-m) boxes on an A-train doubles rig. Overhead loading gantry is typical of those installed at rail terminals.

Similarly there are the cases of container theft, for many high-value loads are handled in this way and the boxes are usually quite plain and give no clue as to their contents – they might contain jewels or jam. There is no doubt also that empty containers make very good storage units once they are repainted and there is even a story of them being spirited away from a dock at the dead of night by a small army of natives who took them to the jungle, cut holes in the roof and rapidly turned the humble containers into the most (locally) desirable residences!

There is little doubt that the introduction of freight containers to the world of international transport has been instrumental in promoting far greater efficiency in these days of highly competitive business. What is incontestable is that these freight boxes are now found in every far-flung corner of the world and the container has become synonymous with efficient multi-modal transport.

Although containers are almost identical the world over, the only differences being identification markings and colour, the vehicles used to haul them overland vary tremendously. To study the numbers of boxes in use in different areas can perhaps give some indication as to the volume of finished goods moving internally and for export. As an example, it is estimated that while there are 1.5 million containers (TEUs or twenty-foot equivalent units) in use in the USA, less than 50,000 ISO units are to be found in the USSR. The inference is either that the Soviets prefer their own type of container, or that fewer consumer goods are moved there. In fact, both these statements are true, the bulk of Soviet freight movement being raw materials which have no need to be moved in containers. Similarly, Israel – a country renowned for its high levels of productivity and its exports – boasts as many freight boxes as France and Italy, despite its infinitely smaller population.

The two biggest container ports in the world are New York and Rotterdam, each of which handles the movement of over 2 million TEUs per year. As might be expected, these areas have high densities of trucks which move the containers between the dock area and the final destination.

The Netherlands has always handled a large portion of Europe's freight and its current weight laws suggest that the Dutch government understands, to some extent, the problems facing its country's truckers. A generous 50-tonnes gross is permitted, provided the requisite number of axles are on the road, and even this limit can be exceeded in some cases if individual axle loadings are not exceeded. A four-axle rigid, hauling a three-axle drawbar, for example, although technically restricted to a maximum gross of 50 tonnes, can gross up to 55 tonnes if both truck and trailer are carrying 20-ft (6-m) containers *and* axle loadings are legal.

This apparently bizarre situation stems from a tacit understanding that containers invariably weigh more than their documents say they do! Most hauliers, at one time or another, have encountered freight boxes which are grossly overweight, some reporting that amounts double that shown on accompanying paperwork have been foisted on to unsuspecting truckers. So, in order to at least reduce the chances of a costly axle-overload fine, Dutch truckers

specialising in the movement of 20-ft (6-m) boxes have grasped the nettle and opted for expensive – and weighty – 4 + 3 truck-trailer combinations. This approach offers the best flexibility, but not the best payload, a 3 + 3 or 4 + 2 scoring heavily here. Nevertheless, the eight-wheeler and three-axle drag is an increasingly popular layout in the Netherlands and these impressive rigs, hauled mostly by DAF, Terberg, MAN or Scania, are a welcome sight indeed to those who believed the artic (or tractor-trailer rig) would replace entirely the more aesthetic heavy truck-trailer combination.

Further evidence of the effectiveness of the four-axle truck and three-axle trailer for moving containers is found in Sweden, where one company, Ramstroms Akeri, operates a Volvo F12 8 × 2 with a Scandi demount system specifically designed to cope with the unpredictable weights frequently encountered.

Interestingly, Sweden's maximum gross weight of 51.4 tonnes corresponds closely to that prevailing in the Netherlands but, whereas the Dutch allow a gross of 32.2 tonnes on an 8 × 2 truck, Sweden permits a rather surprisingly modest 26.24 tonnes. The solution being sought by operators in both countries is, however, identical, with the objective being to reduce the chances of overloading when carrying two 20-ft (6-m), ISO containers on truck-trailer combinations.

Soviet doubles rigs are extremely rare but can be found occasionally hauling twin tanks or container trailers. This Kamaz combination is hauling both ISO and Soviet-built boxes.

In Ramstrom's experience, 20-ft (6-m) containers gross about 15 tonnes, making it virtually impossible to haul them legally with a three-axle truck (the most common configuration in Sweden), although they are easily accommodated on three-axle trailers which can gross a much more useful 30 tonnes. But by using an 8 × 2 truck at the front end of the rig, Ramstroms can haul two 15-tonne boxes, one on the actual truck body and one on the trailer. The solution is not perfect since about 5 tonnes of payload potential is unused but, within the framework of Swedish legislation, there are few alternatives that work as well.

Ramstrom's work flow is such that their container haulage peaks out for fairly short periods and, when the slump occurs, more conventional long-distance traffic is undertaken. But, whatever the reasons behind the design of this unusual truck, its visual impact is considerable, most Swedish truckers doing a quick 'double-take' as the 8 × 2 'S' ride flashes by. A smart machine when solo, its overall appearance when hooked to the three-axle trailer is nothing short of stunning. A few problems with stability towards the rear end of the truck had been anticipated but, by

New Zealand's roads carry large numbers of British-built vehicles in addition to those from Japan and the USA. The Scammell Crusader was popular before the current 'S' series and Road Train took over as this interesting eight-wheeler container-truck shows.

placing the rear axles as far rearward as possible, this was eliminated and the result is a truck that is effective in operation and a delight to handle.

Although we have looked at two examples of truck-trailer rigs hauling containers, more commonplace perhaps is the artic, or tractor-trailer combination, on which skeletal chassis are employed in the interest of weight saving. Skeletals or dual-purpose trailers are undoubtably the most efficient and widely used vehicles for moving ISO freight boxes and these are fitted with easily adjusted twist locks which secure the container to them. Combinations of 10-, 20-, 30- or 40-footers (equivalent to 3, 6, 9 and 12 m) may be loaded on to trailers – the obvious restrictions involve

Arrow Transportation of Vancouver operate a small fleet of purpose-built Freightliner tractors coupled to Knight B-train doubles. Unique feature is fuel tanks (not for the truck) mounted over neck of trailer.

length limits and both gross and axle weights, as mentioned in the case of the truck-trailer.

In Europe, a short-wheelbase two-axle tractor, coupled to a tri-axle semi-trailer is the most frequently encountered outfit while, on the other side of the Atlantic, the preference is for a three-axle tractor and tandem-trailer. In some areas of North America, special doubles combinations have been devised to haul two 20-ft (6-m) boxes and, to European eyes, these rigs seem unnecessarily lengthy and complex. The reasons behind these layouts, however, generally concern the weight of the laden boxes and the only method of coping with two heavy, although short, boxes, is to spread the load over several groups of axles in an A or B train format.

When talking of containers, it is also assumed – sometimes in error – that loading/unloading mechanisms are available at all sites to lift the boxes on and off the chassis. Certainly most modern docks have incredibly efficient cranes, straddle-carriers and similar machinery capable of handling and stacking the vast numbers of boxes arriving each day. Similarly, rail terminals have acquired such equipment. Problems arise at small, often remote, locations which cannot justify the capital expenditure required to purchase cranes used perhaps two dozen times a year. In such cases, the answer sometimes is to rig up a simple overhead gantry or, as is more common nowadays, to utilise a special trailer-mounted container-loading device which can lift any ISO box on and off a trailer.

Such devices are now often used in the USSR, one country which, as already mentioned, has been slow to adopt the ISO container. This approach is understandable when it is remembered that not only is the country absolutely vast, but that its road-transport system is lagging 10 to 15 years behind that of the industrialised West.

It is also significant, perhaps, that the Soviets have

a definite preference for truck-mounted cranes and far greater numbers of these are found in the USSR than in any other country. Again the reason is that these may be used to move freight, but are also capable of loading and unloading it.

Here it is necessary to explain that, while building materials, such as concrete sections for apartment blocks, bricks, timber and aggregate, are carried loose in tippers or dropside vehicles, consumer freight is moved in non-ISO crates built of timber or steel. These are found in abundance throughout the USSR and, although many are in a poor condition, they doubtless provide some deterrent to the pilferage that might otherwise occur as a result of the short supply of desirables such as electrical goods or cosmetics. These crates are hauled in the back of dropside trucks, on step-frame semi-trailers or, indeed, on almost any vehicle and their numbers far exceed those of the standard ISO box. Models such as the Maz 500 and 6000 series, the little Kaz 608 and Kolhida, the

mighty Kraz 257, the Kamaz and ubiquitous Zil 130 are all found transporting these Soviet crates, although the task of loading or unloading them frequently falls to the heavier vehicles mentioned, such as the Kraz or Maz types.

Still on the subject of non-standard containers, we find that some operations call for boxes built to exact dimensions in order to meet the requirements of a specific job.

A case in point concerns Arrow Transportation of Vancouver in Western Canada, an innovative trucking company, with separate divisions for mining, heavy hauling, highway and bulk commodities, which even has its own ships. Recently, Arrow designed and had built a number of B-train rigs specifically required for one operation for a particular customer. The seemingly insuperable problem involved hauling over 36 million litres (8 million Imperial gallons) of fuel northbound from Vancouver to Stewart in marine barges and thence to an isolated asbestos

mine in Cassiar, a town located almost 560 km (350 miles) to the east and accessible only via a gravel highway.

The return haul from the mine to Stewart represented the more difficult run, since 45 tonnes of asbestos fibre had to be moved in containers which were absolutely weatherproof and which would not allow the harmful contents to leak out. In all, the contract called for a total of 66,000 tonnes of asbestos to be hauled back to Stewart and then down the coast again by barge.

Specifying the combination capable of fulfilling the two roles required of it was a challenging task, but Arrow's experts, in conjunction with L. Knight – a specialist body builder – put together an eight-axle B-train which met all the criteria. The result is a rig 22.8 m (75 ft) in overall length, 2.6 m (8 ft 6 in) wide, 4 m (13 ft) high and capable of grossing 63.5 tonnes (140,000 lb). Power is provided by a 475-hp Detroit Diesel, transmission is a fifteen-speed Fuller with 27.2

tonnes (60,000 lb) Rockwell bogie drive axles. All axle loadings are kept legal by dint of having containers of different lengths, the first being 17 ft 6 in (5.3 m) long and designed to haul nineteen bundles of asbestos and the second slightly larger, being 21 ft (6.4 m) inside and built for twenty-two bundles.

Both containers are carried on skeletal trailers and have provision for loading and unloading by a huge forklift at one end of the haul and overhead crane at the other. In addition, the leading trailer has two 5,455-litre (1,200-Imperial gallon) tanks mounted on its chassis, while the rearmost has one such tank. In essence, 16,365 litres (3,600 Imperial gallons) of fuel are hauled by each rig into the mine, together with other essential supplies and, on each return trip, 45 tonnes of asbestos are moved. While this alone may not sound particularly impressive, perhaps it should be mentioned that the terrain crossed on the 560-km (350-mile) trip is reckoned to be the toughest in North America – winter temperatures plummet to −45°C (−50°F) and snowfall can accumulate to a total depth of over 9 m (30 ft) in one season!

All things considered, the Arrow B-trains probably provide one of the best possible examples of how non-standard containers in the Western world contrast absolutely with their Soviet counterparts in terms of efficiency and capacity.

Yet another type of container is the tank unit, which is basically a cylindrical or elliptical tank housed within an ISO framework, which may be loaded, stacked or hauled in exactly the same way as a standard freight container. These units have grown in popularity in recent years as the need to transport specialised liquid commodities has expanded and, nowadays, it is not uncommon to see tanks many thousands of miles from their home base and on the back of a truck or trailer which would probably be unidentifiable to the residents of the country concerned.

F or use at remote locations where the need to transfer ISO boxes seldom arises, it is possible for the carrying vehicle to be equipped with its own unloading gear.

Considering the almost legendary efficiency with which the ingenious and dedicated Japanese are credited, it comes as a great surprise to learn that their road-transport system is so beset with rules and regulations that it is almost a miracle that any 'large' loads, including containers, are moved at all.

As always, there are reasons and, with the Japanese, it is apparent that their entire life style is governed by a recognition that their most valuable and scarcest commodity is space. Japan is a tiny country when one considers the population of almost 110 millions and it was acknowledged years ago that, if such huge numbers of people were to co-exist successfully, then strict rules were essential in order to control behaviour.

Needless to say, when regulations were drawn up and handed out, the trucking industry received its fair share. Legislation extended to cover everything from the minimum performance of laden trucks on uphill grades to rear-view vision mirrors and anti-underrun protection.

Most Japanese trucks are very small, the largest grossing a modest 20 tonnes, unless a special operating permit allows a higher weight! The most popular vehicle for the unrestricted maximum is the rigid six-wheeler, this most probably featuring twin-steer front axles and a single-drive rear. Other layouts are also found, including a more conventional 6 × 2 with a trailing axle located behind the drive axle. On this arrangement, either twin wheels or a single wheel and tyres are mounted on the dead axle.

The 20-ft (6-m) ISO containers are easily hauled on the six-wheelers, many of which boast a remarkably

A bulk salt tank within an ISO frame being lowered onto a skeletal trailer after being trucked from the salt works by rail. It is interesting that a notice on the space frame around the tank forbids the stacking of this particular container.

long wheelbase, but of course 30- and 40-footers (9- and 12-m containers) require the use of a tractor-trailer. Since the maximum overall length for any vehicle is set at a restrictive 40 ft (12 m), this again results in problems. Operators wishing to haul 'overlength' loads require a special permit and the frequency of such applications must keep the bureaucracy of the transport department at full stretch.

Almost 5,000 million tonne-kilometres of freight were moved in Japan during 1984, the vast majority going by road or via coastal shipping. Evidence of the bias towards smaller vehicles is provided by the fact that there are almost 50,000 non-ISO freight containers with a 5-tonne capacity in use and only 1,000 offering 10 tonnes. The smaller boxes are not fitted with twist locks but are secured to the deck of the vehicle by a short chain. A recess in the centre of the box on the underside accommodates the tongues of forklifts which carry out the loading and unloading.

Dimensions of the 5-tonne container are $8 \times 8 \times 12$ ft ($2.4 \times 2.4 \times 3.7$ m) so it is in length only that it differs from its ISO counterpart. But there are still problems with this container, despite its shorter length, these resulting from a 12 ft 6 in (3.8 m) overall height limit on all Japanese motorway-class roads. The solution has been to keep the platform height of the truck as low as possible and this has been done with low profile tyres and, on the latest vehicles, variable-height air suspension.

I In order to conform to complex 'Bridge Formula' weight restrictions, North American trucks hauling containers often appear unnecessarily complicated to European eyes. Here two 20-footers are hauled on a Canadian A-train double.

With a little over 99% of all its crude oil supplies imported, it is little wonder that Japan's truck operators have become increasingly concerned with fuel efficiency in recent years. Containers are not exactly aerodynamic and there is little that can be done to make them so, but cab-mounted air foils, under-bumper skirts and a variety of fairings on the vehicles themselves are fast finding acceptance with today's operator. It is a shame then that the advantages provided by these components are offset to some extent by the veritable forest of mirrors sprouting forward from any heavy truck and the stiff power-to-weight requirement.

There are certainly some massively powerful engines currently in production, with Isuzu offering a 390-hp V12 in its 810 series vehicles and a 340-hp V10 air-cooled diesel from Nissan. These are the latest in a line of power plants developed not only to meet the power requirements of the domestic market but to further advance the Japanese thrust into markets such as Australia, where early Japanese diesels enjoyed limited success in the really heavy end of the weight range. It seems likely that, once these engines have proved themselves sufficiently powerful and reliable in markets outside of Japan, the next stage will be to re-tune in the interests of fuel efficiency.

There is much conjecture about Japan's talent for producing a product ideally suited to a wide variety of markets, but its own truck industry is so different from

The eight-wheeler concept is not common in Sweden, legislation there favouring three-axle trucks and three or four-axle full-trailers. However, problems with overloaded containers encouraged one operator to adopt this unusual configuration. A Scandi demount allows rapid turn around and truck is a Volvo 8 × 2 'S' ride.

A special cigar-shaped tank adequately braced within its ISO frame seen heading to its destination on a Ferrymasters skeletal trailer, hauled by one of their rear-steer Mercedes tractors acquired when the fleet was uprated to 38-tonne operation.

that of Europe and North America that it seems unlikely that Japanese vehicles, at the heavier end of the scale, will make the inroads into these markets so often forecast. Certainly the current generation of cabs are comfortable, if a little fussy, and transmission/axle combinations seem both reliable and well engineered. Engine development, however, is some way behind that of market leaders in the West, such as Cummins or Gardner, and high-torque diesels giving long life is not an area in which the Japanese have much experience. The situation might change but, at present, any invasion by Japanese products will probably be restricted to small vehicles.

MOVING THE LIVESTOCK

'Cattle haulers have it easy. The load walks itself on at one end and off at the other.' Such comments are often heard out on the road but, of course, although the idea may be right, the reality is far from the truth.

Hauling livestock is far from being a simple task and truckers specialising in this particular type of load are a special breed, possessing not only the skills required to drive trucks but also a built-in understanding of animals, which includes recognising sickness and disabilities and coping with the various feeding habits (and inevitable end products resulting from this) of several different species. Anyone not convinced that handling animals is a talent in itself should try their hand at loading 400 lb (180 kg) of irate pig or even an evasive ewe determined not to leave the protection of the flock.

The origins of hauling livestock are easy enough to understand. At one time, cattle, pigs or sheep raised on farms or smallholdings were taken short distances to the nearest town for sale, either to butchers' shops of other farmers. If the farm was too remote to allow

Sadly Leader trucks are no longer built in Australia, but many continue to give good service. Pictured in New Zealand is this 8 × 4 plus tri-axle trailer hauling a triple-deck load of sheep.

Huge 'possum-belly' semi-trailers are used in North America to haul large numbers of cattle or sheep from farm to processing plant. Biggest problem facing the driver is limited ground clearance of the trailers and overall height.

Since its takeover by Paccar, Foden has widened its driveline options considerably. Pictured in New Zealand is a 6 × 4 livestock truck powered by a Caterpillar 3406B rated at 350 hp.

the animal to walk in to town on its own four feet, then a small waggon was employed to carry it. Farms were small, productivity levels were low ('intensive farming' had yet to surface) and the amount of livestock travelling any distance at all was minimal.

Meanwhile, in countries such as Australia, New Zealand, the USA and Canada, a different sort of farming was developing. In these areas, the emphasis was on high volumes and herds of range cattle grew as large as 3,000 head in the most productive regions. In the era of the cowboy, these huge herds were driven on the hoof across the plains to the nearest cattle station, but the resulting problem was simple enough to perceive. What use was it to allow cattle to graze and fatten for several months if the same animals lost most of this newly acquired weight *en route* to the point of sale?

At first it was the railways that cornered the livestock-hauling business in the New World countries but, as road networks developed and trucks in-

creased in size and improved in reliability, so farmers gradually transferred at least part of the task of hauling their animals to trucks. As always, the advantages included a door-to-door service and the entire operation was usually under the control of one man, the driver.

Livestock trucks today come in a variety of shapes and sizes, depending upon the job required of them and the distances over which they are required to operate. A typical European livestock vehicle is a two- or tri-axle rigid, having one or two decks and equipped with a counterbalanced tail-gate at the rear which serves as a loading/unloading ramp for the livestock being transported. In recent years, the bodywork has changed from wooden construction to aluminium, in the interests of weight and serviceability. Hygiene standards are important if contagious disease is to be avoided and it is far easier to keep an aluminium box sparkling than wooden versions, which are prone to absorb microbes and odours.

Drivers of this class of vehicle are expected to have an intimate knowledge of farms in the region and an innate ability to handle any type of animal. It is taken for granted that reversing your truck down a narrow country lane into a farmyard before dawn will in itself present no problem.

Long-haul livestock hauliers are a slightly different breed to the 'local boys' and are found in countries such as the USA and Australia. These truckers handle their big 'possum belly' semi-trailers (often referred to as 'cattle-liners') with a casual indifference that often betrays their farming backgrounds. Most grew up on farms and quickly learned, as does any farm lad, how to drive the latest machine, in addition to knowing

In recent years, the old style, heavy coach-built livestock bodywork has given way to lighter, more durable light-alloy sectional bodies which have the advantage of being easier to keep clean.

instinctively how to look after animals. For these people, trucking long distances, feeding their charges and ensuring their delivery unharmed and unruffled is almost second nature. Electric cattle prods are regarded with outright scorn by the professional cattle haulier, most of whom rely on a well-trained and wily dog to deal with any difficult beast.

There can be problems, even for the most experi-

Soviet road transport is generally poorly organised and equipped, with little in the way of sophistication. Here a Kraz 257 tractor hauls a surprisingly modern livestock semi-trailer, but there is only one deck and little protection is afforded to the cattle.

enced cattle hauler. A steer (bullock) that decides to lie down stands the risk of being trampled to death, while sheep and pigs can die from heart attacks if over-excited. Similarly, chickens will cluster together if frightened and many will die from suffocation as a result. The clever chicken haulier knows that if a load of live chickens suddenly decide to rush *en masse* from one side of their crates to the other, the truck carrying them will keel over like a yacht in a hurricane, so it is best to be prepared. In short, there is nothing predictable about the business of livestock hauling.

Horses are a different matter, representing as they do, the elite, up-market end of the animal world. In keeping with this image, horse 'boxes' are frequently designed in such a way that their cargo is transported in cosseted luxury. Indeed, many horse boxes nowadays feature extravagant living accommodation, not only for the four-legged equines, but for their owners and riders. Air conditioning, stereo systems and even built-in bars are all part and parcel of today's horse box. It is still important to do well in the riding events, of course, but almost as important to be seen arriving in the latest version of a particularly classy horse box. The value of these expensive vehicles is recognised by many truck manufacturers who sponsor the best riders and contribute to the cost of the horse box for the privilege of having the chassis seen at all the best equestrian events around Europe. Renault, Mercedes, Volvo, Ford and Bedford chassis are those most often used in the UK which is where the high-class, high-cost horse box has its biggest following.

BULK IT!

One has only to hear the word 'bulker' and immediately the image of a heavy, rugged vehicle used for hauling rubble or heavy aggregate springs to mind. Trucks used in this sector of the market are heavy duty all the way, specifications including tough, resilient suspension systems and deep-reduction gearing. There is, after all, little point in operating a vehicle in which the components will not stand up to the rigours of shock-loading from huge mechanical shovels or where the overall gear ratios will not permit fully laden operation across soft and treacherous construction sites. Chassis-frame rails come in for special attention too, these being reinforced with flitchplates along part or all of their length. Similarly the bodywork has to be carefully chosen, with the operator selecting the material, tipping gear, size and type of construction, depending on the job or jobs the vehicle will have to perform. It is not only aggregate that is carried in bulkers, but commodities such as grain, flour, sand, salt and foodstuffs such as root vegetables or apples for pressing. Because each type of load has its own qualities, different bodywork may be required for different cargoes.

Rigid trucks are generally those employed on short-haul work and these may be two-, three- or four-axle machines. Mechanical specifications vary from country to country and there are no real hard-and-fast rules that can be applied to describe the appearance of the 'typical' tipper or dump-truck; it probably is fair to say that the three-axle version with double-drive bogie and 18–20-ft (5.5–6-m) alloy body designed to carry most types of material used in the construction business is most people's idea of such a vehicle.

Staying with this particular class of vehicle for a moment we find, as expected, that operators from different parts of the globe have their own ideas as to how the finished product should look.

North America favours the conventional (bonneted) look and trucks such as Mack's DM and Kenworth's C-500 series are still preferred to the cabover (forward-control) trucks offered by these manufacturers, despite the problems of getting sufficient weight onto the front axle. Gross weights for these rugged 6 × 4 dumpers is in the region of 50,000 to 60,000 lb (22.73 to 27.3 tonnes), depending upon the state or province in which they are operated and on items such as tyres and axle spacings. Drive-axle spacings extend from 52 to 72 in (132 to 183 cm) and front axles may be rated anywhere from 10,000 to 21,000 lb (4.5 to 9.55 tonnes), again depending upon the rating of the axle itself and tyre sizes. These trucks are often equipped with hydraulic or air-operated automatic tail-gate controlled from the cab and, on vehicles used in northern regions, where temperatures plummet to unpleasant sub-zero temperatures in winter, exhaust systems are set up to allow the warm gases to circulate in the body, thereby ensuring a clean discharge at the unloading site.

The UK's six-wheel tippers are a very different species to their North American counterparts, being almost exclusively forward control and having a far less rugged appearance. Despite the clean lines of Leyland's Constructor Six and Volvo's F7 (the two bestsellers in the UK, in the three-axle market) the driveline in each case has proved itself more than capable of coping with the wide variety of conditions encountered in the demanding on-off road construction business. Engine power in the 230 to 250-hp range, differential locks and suspensions permitting a high degree of articulation ensure that these trucks carry out the tasks demanded of them with the minimum number of problems for both driver and owner.

Six-wheel rigids may well be representative of bulk vehicles but many other configurations exist. In Scandinavia, huge three-axle rigid trucks haul four-axle trailers and gross up to 70 tonnes in some cases on private road systems. Finland allows 48 tonnes on six axles (as does Denmark) and trucks such as the stylish

Sisu SR 300 8 × 2 haul two-axle trailers effortlessly across the sparsely trafficked highways, thanks to the power provided by diesels such as the Cummins NTE 400-20.

Weight limits in Europe may not equal those in Norseland, but what bulkers there lack in terms of payload they make up for in sheer sophistication. Switzerland's are a delight to behold, the gleaming bodywork and carefully painted trucks reflecting the operator's attention to detail and obvious professionalism.

Mighty eight-wheeler Saurers pound the clean and efficient road network, the quality and durability of the almost silent engine and brilliantly matched driveline undiminished by the rounded, rather dated

The Yugoslavian TAM truck is not often seen outside of its homeland, but features an advanced specification on its latest models. An air-suspension system for the cab has been introduced but is not yet in full production. Here model 260T26 receives a load.

lines of the cab. These same vehicles will still be working in 20 years' time and it is a tragedy that Saurer no longer builds these exquisitely engineered trucks. It remains to be seen if the big 3333 and 3336 Mercedes tippers destined to replace them will last as well.

Gross vehicle weights are not high in Switzerland, the maximum for an eight-wheeler being 28 tonnes, but, despite this restrictive limit, there is no compromise when it comes to working out the specification of the complete truck. The power-to-weight ratio demands an engine capable of producing at least 280 hp but, in practice, this figure is exceeded to a generous degree. Volvo, DAF, Scania and Mercedes all offer engines in excess of 330 hp and these are widely used. Gearboxes and axles need to be compatible with these high-output diesels and the net result is inevitably a fairly weighty chassis and cab.

To compound this disadvantage, all the bodywork used in Switzerland is extremely sophisticated. Most tippers are of the three-way variety and may tip off either side of the vehicle as well as off the back.

Attractive Alusuisse aluminium is extensively employed in both the superstructure itself and for items such as rear wings and catwalks, but the weight saving is not enough to reduce the overall tare of a completed eight-wheel bulk-tipper down beneath 12 or 13 tonnes. Additional features, such as electromagnetic retarders, air-operated power tail-gates and even demount body systems reduce payloads still further but, nevertheless, are frequently used for reasons of safety and convenience.

In almost total contrast to the smooth sophistication which identifies the trucks used in Switzerland, rugged 'utilitarianism' is the term which best describes the bulk trucks used by Soviet and Eastern bloc countries. Russian-built Kraz, Maz and Zil rigids are quite obviously built on the assumption that styling and driver amenities don't appear anywhere on the manufacturer's list of priorities and even the more modern Kamaz can hardly be described as refined. Bodywork is produced in the same factory as the truck chassis and can be matched only to the one model, with the result that specialised trucks are either an ungainly mismatch of components or imported complete from Europe.

Soviet winters are among the harshest on earth and it would be reasonable to assume that truck builders designing equipment capable of withstanding the fierce onslaught of a Siberian blizzard would have the job right by now. In fact, the majority of the vehicles working in the bleakest, most remote areas are Tatras built in Czechoslovakia and, although they may lack the style and finish of Western products, they have established a reputation for reliability which is a legend throughout the USSR.

Most of these Tatras are 6×6 tippers which incorporate the highly individualistic features synonymous with the marque, the best known of which is the tubular back-bone chassis on to which all components are hung. Prior to 1979, two basic models

Rugged, but practical, the North American dump-truck presents a no-frills image characterised by this seven-axle truck trailer rig which can legally gross nearly 64 tonnes.

Bedford TM eight-wheelers are not sold in their native UK, but in New Zealand this rare example, powered by a V8 Detroit Diesel, is still in operation. Maximum gross weight for truck-trailer combination is 39 tonnes but moves are afoot to increase this to 44 tonnes soon.

were built: the bonneted 148 and the forward-control 813. A total of fifty-seven versions were produced, largest of which were the impressive 8 × 8 chassis designed for use either as 55-tonne gvw dumpers or heavy haulage motive units.

Today Tatra produces the 815 series in thirty-six versions and this model replaces both earlier types. Improvements over previous models include a tilt cab, longer servicing interval, easier steering and better driver comfort. At present, the 815 is still in the process of establishing itself as the best truck for difficult conditions and impossible climates, but there can be little doubt that it seems likely to become as legendary as its predecessors, and they earned their laurels the hard way. In any case, the future of the 815 was assured from day one, thanks to the East European Council for Mutual Economic Assistance, whose transport committee selected it as *the* 12-tonne plus truck most suitable for operation in Eastern bloc countries. As a result, an incredible 15,000 units per year are hoped for, with 60% of these going for export.

In the same way that many differences exist between the truck types and configurations used in different regions of the world, there exists an enormous and bewildering number of differences in bodywork.

Whatever the load to be carried, the main preoccupation is with loading the vehicle to legal limits.

As a result, bulk bodies on both rigid trucks and semi-trailer chassis are often tapered to allow loads to be concentrated more at one end than another. Interestingly, on forward-control six-wheeler rigid vehicles, it is often necessary to taper the body so that the thick end of the wedge is at the front. Meanwhile, on semi-trailers, the reverse is usually the case, particularly with British 38-tonne combinations employing a two-axle tractor/three-axle trailer approach. In the latter case, it is necessary to load in such a way that the single-drive axle is not overloaded and to transfer weight rearwards on the 22.5-tonne capacity tri-axle bogie on the trailer.

Loading to legal requirements is a never-ending problem for the driver of vehicles engaged on bulk work and, over the years, a number of components have arrived on the scene which claim to make things easier for the hapless tipper operator. On-board axle-load sensors, some providing digital read-outs in the cab, have been available for some years, but the prob-

In Switzerland, operators place great importance on efficiency. Despite a low gross weight of only 28 tonnes, trucks are carefully specified and finished. Side-tippers are the norm and superb examples such as this Steyr eight-wheeler with Lanz and Marti bodywork are commonplace.

lem with these lies in the type of work bulkers perform, work which is dirty, heavy and not conducive to prolonging the life of sophisticated and delicate electronic gadgetry. Air suspension on trailers has been more successful in that, although this in itself obviously provides no security against overloading, it does ensure that each trailer axle is carrying exactly the same amount of weight.

Rigid tipper vehicles in the UK generally employ single ram, front-end-mounted tipping gear to hoist the bulk body but, in Europe and North America, there is a very definite preference for underfloor equipment. Similarly, although three-way tippers are rarely used in the UK, they are found in very large numbers in Europe. Indeed, the Swiss, who are obsessed with efficiency in the same way as the Swedes are with safety, appear to use three-way tipping bodies exclusively. This apparent disregard for additional expense and tare weight is, however, offset to some extent by the fact that the Swiss operator expects (and

apparently receives) total reliability from his truck and utilises them over many years with virtually no unscheduled down-time.

For reasons of traction on soft ground and stability when raising the body, rigid three- and four-axle trucks are preferred to articulated vehicles for the movement of dense loads such as aggregate. That is not to suggest that these vehicles, with their larger capacity, don't have their place in the movement of bulk goods. Far from it, tractor-trailer rigs are favourites for grain, coal, phosphates, minerals, sawdust, woodchips, sand, flour, salt and a host of other free-flowing materials. As with all other types of truck, the layout will be determined by various factors, including the local legislation, length of haul, access to loading and unloading facilities, terrain to be negotiated, axle- or gross-weight taxation structure and so forth.

If tipping a load off cannot be accomplished, then other methods of discharge have to be employed and these can involve utilising a gravity-fed bottom-hopper or belly-dump body, powered systems, such as augers, or perhaps sophisticated sucking and blowing equipment.

These devices may be driven by a gearbox-mounted power-take-off (pto) or by an independent donkey engine and the most sophisticated systems, when fitted

$\mathbf{D}$AF 3300 6 × 4 and tri-axle grain-trailer epitomise the scene in the rural Netherlands. Truck employs underfloor gear while the trailer has a front-end ram. An air-suspended lift axle is fitted to the trailer for empty running.

to specialised bodywork, represent a very large financial investment.

Yet another method of unloading, seldom used in Europe but frequently employed in the USA (particularly on the West Coast) is that where a laden vehicle is driven on to a huge ramp which is then raised, using hydraulic rams, to a point where the load is dumped off the read end. This method is used by large companies whose trucks are able to carry more payload by virtue of the fact that no tipping mechanism is fitted to the vehicle itself. There is also no question of a truck ever turning over while unloading, since the complete rig is safely secured to the elevating ramp.

This process is frequently employed by sawmill operators whose woodchip bulkers are extremely tall and have a high centre of gravity, making them inherently unstable. A recent development with 'chip-haulers' is the B-train 'dump-thru' system in which twin-trailers coupled in B-train style are raised on ramps and the leading semi-trailer dumps its load off through the rearmost trailer using the rear doors as 'sides' joining the two units. In this way, discharge time is substantially reduced; previous methods required the rearmost trailer to be emptied before the load in the lead unit could be dumped off.

Weight saving is always an important consideration and truckers as far afield as Finland and America's West Coast use a similar method to attain this important goal on their truck-trailer combinations. In this instance, tipping gear is installed on the truck but not on the trailer. Instead, the trailer body is winched off its chassis and forward into the truck body (assuming this has already been dumped of course!) and the tipping mechanism on the truck also empties the trailer. To those unfamiliar with the system, it sounds both slow and unnecessarily complicated but, in practice, it works well. Although the body-transfer system cannot possibly be as rapid as tipping off a big semi-trailer, the loads carried can be

as big and stability is far better, so there are tangible benefits. Normal configuration for a 'transfer-box' rig from California comprises a long-wheelbase conventional 359 Peterbilt or Kenworth W900 coupled to a fairly short tandem-axle pup trailer. As may be expected, the trucks are heavily chromed and, by European standards, appear to be very over-spec'd for the task required of them. As already mentioned, a long-bonneted truck seems an odd choice for a tipper, especially when one considers the difficulties of putting enough load on to the steering axle.

Another oddity concerns the length of the drawbar tongue or A-frame used to couple the truck and trailer. In many instances, this appears to be at least 20 ft (6 m) in length, longer than the trailers themselves. Car drivers certainly need to be alert when driving alongside one of these combinations since the

$\mathbf{I}$n some areas, a swap-body system is used by dump-truck operators in order to reduce the weight and cost penalty incurred when hydraulic-tipping gear is fitted to both truck and trailer. This method is widely used in Finland and is splendidly illustrated by this magnificent Sisu SR 300 8 × 2 truck-and-trailer combination.

Sawdust is a bulky but fairly lightweight commodity so the trailers hauling this load tend to be very tall. Here an Australian Kenworth takes on a load at a sawmill.

drawbar, in addition to being deceptively long, is also very low-slung. As a result, it is impossible to see the actual drawbar if it is beside you on your blind side but not impossible to feel that you can nip in between the truck ahead and the vehicle behind it, not realising the two are connected!

The mid-western part of Canada and the USA is often referred to as 'The World's Bread Basket' so vast is the area and so enormously productive its endless grain farms. The prairies are an awesome size and, over the years, have provided quantities of wheat, oats, barley and other cereals that have helped feed the hungry of both Eastern and Western cultures.

Traditionally, grain was harvested and trucked short distances to skyscraper-tall 'elevators', where it was graded and stored prior to being loaded on to lengthy railroad 'grain trains' which, in turn, unloaded into ocean-going ships at coastal ports. Long-distance grain hauls by truck were not considered viable and, indeed, the service offered could not compete with that of the rail system, which boasted a depot in every small community and the facility to make up a 100-car freight train solely for grain transport whenever the necessity arose.

But things have been changing in recent years as the railways have cut back on expenditure and gradually closed down many seldom-used and therefore non-profitable branch lines. As the rail network has contracted, so the trucking industry has been quick to expand in order to take up the slack.

Today, sleek, modern, highway 'grain trains' take the strain out of cereal haulage. Large, efficiently operated fleets of tractor-trailers have replaced the small farm truck and, even on long distance hauls from the mid-west to ports such as Vancouver or Seattle, trucks have proved themselves cheaper and quicker.

Evidence that highway haulage of bulk grains is a recent phenomenon is provided by L. E. Matchett Trucking of Saskatchewan, a company that started in

Possibly the smartest and most unusual truck in Switzerland is this exquisite White Road Commander. Converted from a tractor unit to an 8 × 2, the truck features a self-steering rear axle and bulk-blower body. Operated by Julius Tschopp of Lucerne, the truck was converted by the White importer in Lyss.

the bulk business in a modest way as recently as 1974 and today operates eighty-seven units. Matchett hauls throughout western Canada and provides a high level of service to customers as far away as Oregon to the west and Minnesota and Kansas to the east.

International, Freightliner and Peterbilt tractors form the basis of the Matchett operation while trailers are from Lodeking, Doonan, Chamberlain, Marquez and Wellco. Maximum gtw for the bottom-hopper A-train combinations is 53.5 tonnes offering a nett payload of almost 40 tonnes. Any dry product is hauled, examples being fertiliser, grains, livestock feed and potash. B-train tanker combos haul loads of anhydrous ammonia.

Caterpillar and Cummins diesels are used in every truck in the fleet but, of the eleven trucks purchased in 1985, all had Cummins 400 as power plants. These engines, installed in IH 9670 units and Pete 362s, have proved themselves exceptionally reliable in operation and offer good fuel returns. Transmissions are Fuller 15-speed units and drive axles are 20-tonne Eaton 44DS assemblies. All vehicles are equipped with Budd aluminium wheels and Michelin low-profile tyres.

The immaculate blue, white and chromium vehicles operated by Matchett present an unforgettably brilliant picture when outlined against the 'big sky' of the Canadian prairies. But the tractor-trailers are far from being just showpieces and their productivity is closely monitored. Road-speed governors restrict top speed to 90 kph (56 mph) and Argo tachograph charts are sent 2,900 km (1,800 miles) to Toronto, Ontario, once a month for detailed analysis by a specialist. Once processed, the charts reveal a wealth of information, including not only basic speed and driving time, but smooth and progressive gear-shifting both up and down the box and effective use of the engine brake. Fuel consumption is said to be 'impressive' by both drivers and managers and, in addition to

receiving excellent wages and being supplied with top flight equipment, drivers can earn an extra 3 cents a mile for 'good driving techniques'. At 160,000 km (100,000 miles) a year, that adds up to a useful $3,000 bonus, not bad for doing a job that is not impossible to do correctly in the first place.

Aluminium and fibreglass are used extensively in lightweight western-style trailers designed for the movement of grain and other bulk commodities, but one company, based in Utah, has been successfully experimenting for the past 7 years with bonded plywood reinforced with fibreglass (FRP).

The W. S. Hatch Company decided to have its huge coal-hauling trailers built in FRP because inner surfaces were unusually smooth and joint-free, allowing perfect discharge. There was also a useful weight saving and some idea of how important this aspect is to Hatchco is supplied by the fact that their trailers are built without landing legs! Operating with special authority in the neighbouring states of Utah and Nevada, Hatchco's nine-axle twin-trailer rigs gross 59.5 short tons (54 tonnes). Each bottom-dump semi-trailer features a tapered 38 yd³ (29 m³) body and a semi-automatic system for tarping the load. A variety of tractors are used, all of which are specified in the interests of economy and low tare weight. Present preference is for Peterbilt and Freightliner units powered by Detroit Diesels, but there is constant search for lighter, more fuel-efficient combinations. Coal, like any other fuel, has to be extracted from the ground and transported as cheaply as possible, otherwise these processes end up costing more than the value of the load itself. It remains to be seen what interesting developments will next emerge from the Hatch Company's transport operations and, indeed, what changes to materials and configurations will occur in the next decade as operators around the world scramble to find even more efficient ways to haul product.

PAINT YOUR WAGON!

In the first half of the 1980s, trucking in Europe has not been easy and a lot of hauliers have experienced very tough times, battling with bankruptcies that have crippled them financially, sometimes for the rest of their lives. Also due to the economic hardships, many unfortunate drivers have lost their jobs and the same happened to many workers in the truck manufacturing industry. Operators who *did* stay in business have had to put up with several strikes by, among others, customs personnel and dockworkers, plus of course the notorious French blockades that made the trucker's nightmare complete.

However, despite the difficult times in the transport industry for nearly everyone, a small but increasing number of owner-drivers has managed to change the face of trucking on Euro highways dramatically. These are the men who are spending mega-bucks on customising their workhorses and give the industry that much-needed image boost.

Truck festivals have become major events all over Europe, where proud truckers gather together showing off their equipment to fellow men and the general public, and most manufacturers have become aware of the importance of these attractions and the willingness of owner-drivers to smarten up their vehicles. Some producers of the heavy brigade have even come to sponsor complete special custom trucks to take part in festival competitions but, though these machines always look very impressive and glamorous, they can not be called working rigs. These trucks are just sitting there to attract the public and try to catch some of the exposure in the media.

However, some of these expensive units might eventually end up in the hands of a successful owner-operator with enough cash, once the vehicle has done its part on the various trade stands, and not surprisingly the manufacturers can tell you that purchase inquiries are received throughout the events. The enthusiasm for customising commercial vehicles originated several years back when the movie-companies brought out spectacular action-packed truck films like *Convoy* and *Smokey and the Bandit*, glorifying the free spirit of the modern longhaul trucker in his mighty and colourful big rig. Especially on the Continent, many ordinary company drivers wanted to imitate the American 'macho' image from the movies and fitted chromed air horns, US licence plates, little flags and dozens of gaudy decals to their working machines.

Many of these heavily adorned vehicles could never come close to looking like a real Kenworth, Peterbilt or Mack and some drivers just managed to achieve the opposite; their vehicles looked pretty ridiculous sometimes and much overdone.

Fortunately for everybody, most European truckers have come to the conclusion that customising should either be done in a big way or abandoned completely.

A lot of drivers, mostly those employed by companies operating mediocre equipment, argue against the custom-truck fraternity and proclaim that a commercial vehicle is only intended to do its job at the lowest possible cost without all the fuss. But what is wrong with showing unity and pride in a profession that is of prime importance to all of us around the world? Surely, our industry could do with more respect from the general public and at least road transport at its best is represented by an increasing number of owner-operators who are willing to invest in and maintain the finest equipment money can buy. And quality does not come cheap these days!

It is sad though that, despite all the efforts made by operators to enhance the looks of commercial vehicles on the road, deep-rooted anti-truck feeling still persists, especially in the UK, for which the blame clearly lies with a small group of narrow-minded environmentalists.

On the Continent and in Scandinavia, trucking is now regarded as the lifeline of the nation and, gener-

ally, more recognition for the hardworking truck driver has been gained in the process; without doubt, running clean, extremely goodlooking heavy trucks has helped a lot. In the northern countries, efficiency and cleanliness is the word. Emanuelssons Åkeri of Motala must be one of Sweden's most envied haulage companies, because they operate a fleet of eight big Scanias and Volvos that are all outstandingly good-looking trucks. One of the new 142H Scania 24-m (78 ft 9 in) reefer truck and trailers is driven by Tommy Bengtsson, a very professional trucker who has spent a large amount of his wages and spare time in making his company outfit even better and one of the most eye-catching combos on Swedish roads. The butter-carrying truck combination that is kept in show-truck condition runs daily across the large country at an all up weight of 52 tonnes gcw. Tommy modified the exterior completely, adding chromed dual-exhaust sidepipes, chromed toolboxes, chromed

bumper and huge 'wild bar' and many smaller but important touches, such as driving and marker lights, air horns, Alcoa wheels and colourful striping, together with small but nicely done murals. To top it off, this enthusiastic trucker refurbished the complete interior making it one of the best working places that can be seen on any Euro truck. The rig's outstanding appearance has already earned him many trophies for 'Best Working Truck' and the company image has been boosted enormously, too, so much in fact that Emanuelssons has come to customise all its newly acquired trucks. The company reckons that the extra cash spent on all the trimmings is well worth it. The drivers take much more pride in their equipment and the clients judge the service offered by the quality of the equipment, which can not be better in this case.

That it pays off to customise a heavy truck in some way or other can be seen on any Scandinavian road; every year countless smart new trucks are put into service and an anti-truck lobby is unheard of. Denmark has been one of the forerunners in organising truck shows and, not surprisingly, this little country now houses an amazing number of working super trucks. Many Danish owner-operators possess some real showstoppers based on various Scania, Volvo,

Five years on the road and still looking pristine is this customised big Scania which hauls at 50 tonnes gcw. It never fails to turn heads as it travels the Dutch highways.

Mercedes or Iveco type tractors and trucks. For example, 20-year-old Henrik Guldager is the proud owner of a 6-year-old Volvo F12 which is so fantastically outfitted and well kept that, even with an amazing 750,000 km (466,000 miles) on the clock, it still outshines almost any other working truck in Europe. 'Sweet Candy II' as the tractor is christened, has won dozens of prizes in major 'beautiful truck competitions' in between its regular long distance hauls with a reefer trailer across Europe.

Styles and taste in paint schemes of these Scandinavian trucks differ from those seen in other countries and hard but brilliant colours are favoured up north, with occasionally just a touch of murals and striping. Ample amounts of polished stainless steel or chromed accessories make for a spectacular overall impression of quality and efficiency, features which make Scandinavian trucking so successful and intriguing at the same time. Up until now, maybe due to lack of expertise or the necessary funds or both, not many Brits have been able to rival the foreign chrome addicts, but a fine exception must be David Miller from Therfield, who hauls farm machinery for a living. His Scania 142M 4×2 tractor, with its distinctive blue and grey colours and a host of heavily chromed accessories, is so painstakingly well kept and neatly fitted out, without being 'overdone', that even the Scandinavians could not do better than give it first prizes.

David's truck not only matches the best custom rigs from the outside, but the interior of the cab and sleeper, done in red semi-leather with brass buttons and ornaments throughout, certainly makes this truck unique. David Miller is not yet content and works already on something even more spectacular, which will be the ultimate owner-driver's truck when it hits the road in 1986.

There is an endless list of bright chromed or stainless steel accessories available today from several dozen local and foreign manufacturers for virtually every make of truck, and sometimes many of the shiny goodies can also be ordered as factory-fitted options.

All this fancy hardware not only looks good, but often saves on tare weight, can improve component life, and might very well help to keep the

1980. He was one of the first in the Lowlands to dress up his truck to such an extent, not only to please himself, but also to show the world that trucks can definitely be beautiful.

More than $\frac{1}{2}$ million km (310,000 miles) later, Peter decided in 1984 to look out for something new and even more classy, but genuine American trucks had become out of the question with the very high dollar-exchange rates and customising a new premium Euro truck from the ground up was not cheap either; so at last he opted for rebuilding his faithful workhorse. Now the 6×2 tractor, pulling a tri-axle tanker looks more elegant than ever with its sparkling metallic blue and silver diamond-shaped paint-job, nicely offset by typical Dutch windmill- and polder-landscape scenes applied to both sides of the cab and custom-built sleeper. This successful independent has obviously done the right thing, because the rig has lately won many trophies at home and abroad and the combination still stirs a lot of interest wherever it goes on its daily hauls in the Benelux. Over the last 5 years, hundreds of Dutch truckers spent a fortune on custom bits and pieces to brighten up their vehicles, making driving down the road there a real joy for anybody with an interest in trucking.

One of the most elaborate and classy tractors to appear on the Dutch scene lately has been the 1985 model Volvo F12 Globetrotter of Bertus Ederveen from Nieuwegein, a truck that must rank amongst the most heavily customised working units in all of Europe. The top-spec Globetrotter was modified in 4 months, from a standard 4×2 machine into a dazzling and unparalleled showstopper, with every imaginable chrome option imported from around the

Dutch duo Bertus Ederveen and Harm Speerstra pictured with one of their artistic creations. Working together, they have produced some stunning paint schemes for working trucks.

business going. After all a clean truck usually means a top flight service! Although becoming increasingly popular now with truck drivers, the industry and the public, customising trucks has been familiar to Continental eyes for many years and the Dutch are operating quite a number of 'Americanised' super-trucks.

One of the Netherlands' most admired custom trucks has been the Scania 141 V8 Aerodyne conventional, owned by Peter Kempen and on the road since

Karl-Arne Jakobson operates this fantastic-looking Volvo six-axle outfit on runs between Sweden and Norway. Unlike some of the glaring high-colour trucks seen around today, this one's black and silver livery has an air of efficient reserve about it.

Many fine trucks can be seen in Sweden, but Emanuelssons Akeri of Motala must have one of the most efficient and smart. This prize winning combination has a host of chrome and stainless-steel accessories which save weight and last longer, as well as giving the outfit a touch of individuality.

world by Bertus' friend and partner, Harm Speerstra, a Dutch-American who drives one of the best looking Peterbilt car transporters on the other side of the Atlantic. The dull grey, factory paint-job was changed to a magnificent deep blue metallic, and complemented with a series of murals depicting the Rocky Mountains and North American Indians with their colourful tribal decorations.

Together with the chromed quarter fenders, air-

intake rams, West-Coast mirrors, air horns and rows of marker lights imported from California, the exclusive sun visor, stone-guard and massive Keith bullbar coming all the way from Australia and various locally made, custom-built accessories, this truck really stands out. Decked out as a real beauty, the 'Worldwide Globetrotter' as it was dubbed, is now putting in the miles for 60 hours or more a week, hauling tilts and reefers for the Norfolk Line and, not

This amazingly detailed Danish Volvo F12 has been trucking around for over 6 years and has clocked up in excess of 750,000 km in that time. Looking as though it was straight out of the paint shop, it is a tribute to its owner.

surprisingly, Bertus Ederveen attracts more attention with this flashy rig on the road than the Dutch Royal Family on a day out would do!

It is not just Scandinavian and Dutch trucks that get the custom treatment so often; the French in particular know a thing or two about this new transport phenomenon and operate some of the most fantastically decorated vehicles in the world. Trucks here are real 'works of art' and are often heavily painted in vivid colours, with the most exotic murals applied to all sides of tractors and trailers. It only started 3 years ago, on the French west coast in Brittany, when a couple of well-known 'airbrush' mural painters decided to have a go on the big 'camions' for a change. Today, literally hundreds of French owner-drivers and small companies have had their money-machines transformed into incredible mobile paintings and, on any 'autoroute', one can spot some examples every day of the week.

In a land that revels in such an abundance of spit-'n'-polish trucks, it is hard to pinpoint any as an example, but one of the most applauded units is Michel Gaillard's exceptional cattle semi. Pulled by an impressive K100 Kenworth Aerodyne, the combination, in red, orange and silver, is covered with the most beautiful Wild-West scenes ever seen.

One could ask why all these amazing murals are so much in vogue with the French truckers today. It might have something to do with the ebullient way of life of these Continentals, who are renowned for their enjoyment of gastronomic meals, wine and pretty ladies as no-one else, or it may just be the number of artists who have mastered the technique of airbrush-painting so well and can do it at an affordable price, even for hard-charging money-conscious truckers. Of course, the whole sunny atmosphere in the south is a big help; rust that eats up some cabs within a few years is less of a problem and thus expensive paint-jobs keep their value much longer. Whatever the reason, French roads and the European transport industry in general, have benefited a lot from this new trend. It gives the truckers themselves much more pride and joy in their work and the normal motorist the chance to reconsider his views about 'those dirty big juggernauts' – and that is certainly worth a few bucks!

DOWN IN THE WOODS

Confined to a network of private roads within the world's forests and seldom seen by the general public or, indeed, truck devotees, loggers are among the most spectacular of all heavy trucks.

Not surprisingly, some marques – among them Pacific and Hayes – were bred especially to cope with the fantastically heavy loads and difficult terrain which are part of the everyday business of hauling timber from the stump to the mill or river's edge. Regrettably, Hayes closed down its operations in 1975, leaving Pacific with a clear field in the manufacture of off-highway logging trucks. Such is the nature of the business, however, that, despite having one less competitor to contend with, Pacific has only managed to sell around 200 heavies a year since 1980, and that number includes other trucks destined for oilfield and mining operations.

It would be reasonable to assume that vehicles hauling loads in excess of 100 tonnes up and down steep, unsurfaced roads would rapidly wear out and need replacing. In fact, the reverse is true and logging

Four-axle tractor units are both appealing and practical. This Australian example illustrates the poor conditions encountered once the hard-surfaced highway is left behind.

The hardwood forests of South-East Asia are harvested by trucks such as this six-wheel rigid Fuso. The vehicle does not employ its own truck-mounted crane for loading as is often the case in Europe.

operation today, thanks to a series of engine and/or gearbox changes and a set of new, beefed-up drive axles. With transplants like this going on over the years, it is little wonder that Pacific and other log-truck builders have a hard time selling new vehicles.

But the market for log trucks, although small and highly specialised, is nevertheless hotly competed for by many of the world's truck manufacturers. In North America, thoroughbreds from the stables of Kenworth, Mack, Peterbilt and Western Star compete in the lumber stakes while, in Europe, smaller, more sophisticated but perhaps less impressive versions are built for a job which is really a very different type of operation.

On the West Coast of both the USA and Canada, it is the sheer size of trees, such as the giant *Sequoia* redwoods which dictate the scale of the equipment found there. Trucks standing 12 ft (3.65 m) high and measuring 12 ft (3.65 m) across use mighty V12 diesels for power and such monsters bear little resemblance to their on-highway cousins. The emphasis here is on performance and stamina. Good looks are not even considered, but what the logger lacks in chrome plate, it makes up for in a bewildering array of equipment designed to keep the driver free from risk as he makes the slippery descent with his giant cargo.

A typical driveline for a heavy off-highway logger might comprise a Cummins KTA-525 diesel driving through an Allison Powershift automatic transmission to Clark hub-reduction drive-axles. Almost certainly the transmission would incorporate a lock-up retarder to help out on steep downhill runs but, in addition to this, a supplementary retarder, such as a Parkersburg Hydrobrake, would be fitted and brake drums would be water cooled. Water for the cooling system and the hydrobrake is carried in tanks which double as a headache rack behind the cab.

While enthusing about the size and power of the trucks themselves, it is easy to overlook the drivers of these huge and complex log haulers. Like the equipment they operate, they are a special breed. Not all drivers would want to tie down loads standing well over 20 ft (6 m) high before starting off down difficult and hairy mountain passes at weights that can gross 200 to 300 tonnes! But, to the logger, it is all in a

trucks up to 30 years old are still found in operation with many of the world's major forest companies. The explanation is simply that the big trucks are built to withstand considerable punishment and, although components do wear and are replaced, the basic vehicle remains essentially intact. The result can be a tractor unit which saw its first filtered sunlight in a West-Coast forest in the 1950s but which is still in

day's work, as is changing the odd flat tyre, no mean feat in itself when it is remembered that, on off-road tractors and trailers, sizes are generally 14.00 × 24s!

Vehicles of a similar size and style are also used in Australia and New Zealand and, again, names such as Kenworth and Mack dominate. It is not that European models cannot compete, and, indeed, many are employed by different contractors, but there can be little doubt that the more rugged construction of the North American models pays dividends in a job where 'roads' are tracks and overloading is commonplace. The sophistication of the smooth Europeans just doesn't fit into an environment where brute strength is king. Few vehicles could be as basic as Mack's DM-

800, or as cramped in the cab as KW's C-500, yet in terms of durability these trucks cannot be faulted. It is a fact that these machines, so often described by European journalists as 'primitive', are far better suited to work in the forests than their stylish and ergonomically superior European counterparts.

In Scandinavia, however, the situation is very different. Weights are likely to be in the region of 60 to 70 tonnes and trucks are not expected to last 30 years. Logging is still a tough and demanding task (although it is unlikely that an American log-trucker would see it this way) but there can be no doubt that this type of logging is in a very different class to that carried out on the Pacific West Coast.

Rigid government control throughout Europe and Scandinavia ensures that, even on private logging roads, there is little scope for loads way in excess of those carried on the normal highway network. As a result, the equipment used in the forests of Norway and Sweden is little different to that operating on

hard-surfaced roads and, in terms of mechanical specifications, there is probably no difference whatsoever. As an example, a Volvo F12 six-wheel rigid hauling a four-axle trailer can operate legally at over 50 tonnes on the normal road system in Sweden and is unlikely to ever haul in excess of 70 tonnes, even on private logging roads.

This situation clearly contrasts the basic difference in attitudes to engineering which exist between the European truck builders and those in North America. For whereas even expensive, well engineered trucks, such as Volvo, Scania, Mercedes and DAF, are available with only a limited range of driveline options, all American builders offer a range of models and driveline options which can cover virtually any type of operation in any location.

There is a tendency for European builders to scorn

The big advantage of a private road network is that any size or weight may be hauled. However, it seems unlikely that the Peterbilt tractor at the front end would be capable of negotiating even the slightest grade with a load of such mind-boggling length and weight.

the American 'assemblers' and to assert firmly that a 'matched driveline' is far more durable and reliable than a series of separate components bolted together and housed in any old chassis. But the incontestable facts are that it is impossible, for financial reasons, for every truck maker to engineer each individual component required in a wide-ranging variety of chassis. Volvo and Scania do particularly well in this area, and Mercedes manages to span a weight range extending from 3.5 to 200 tonnes. But Mercedes has also had to resort to using ZF transmissions in most chassis so there can be little doubt that if they are prepared to compromise in gearboxes, they might also find it preferable at some stage to fit 'outside' engines or axles.

Meanwhile, on the other side of the Atlantic, manufacturers such as Paccar offer a range of heavy trucks which includes not only the prestigious high-way haulers, such as Kenworth's 900 and Peterbilt's 359, but highly specialised off-highway loggers, oil-field trucks, mining vehicles and so forth. Paccar don't claim to build it all themselves but what they do claim is that, once they have selected and assembled the separate components, the finished product will do exactly the job required of it and will have a phenomenal lifespan.

Logging vehicles in North America generally comprise a 6×4 tractor unit coupled to one or more trailers, while in Europe and Scandinavia the most

Pictured here in a true working environment, a Peterbilt tractor hauls its giant load of redwoods across a timber bridge. The water tank for cooling brakes is clearly seen behind the cab and the trailer hook-up is also evident.

Evidence that some trucks really are highly specialised is provided here. The Pacific tractor, built in western Canada, is operated by a small company in distant New Zealand. Built in very small numbers, Pacific vehicles are built specifically for the forest industry.

common configuration is that of a straight truck hauling a full trailer.

Looking at North America first, we find that the tractor-trailer rig does not employ a regular fifth-wheel hook-up but is, in fact, connected by means of a pintle hook in the rear crossmember of the tractor. The pole-type trailer is extendable in order to accommodate different log lengths and air/electrical connections are generally carried beneath the pole. Heavy hardwoods, for example, would make up a full load comprising very few, relatively short log lengths, while an equivalent load of soft pine would probably extend forward over the tractor unit and rearward over the tail end of the trailer, even if this were stretched out to its full reach.

Loading is done using big mobile 'skidders' which can grab a bunch of softwood logs, or perhaps one or two large hardwood logs, and position them expertly between the bolsters on the trailer. Where loads have to be carried over the regular highway system, it is necessary to consider axle loadings and overall lengths (including legally permitted overhangs) but, on private logging roads, the philosophy is simply to load to capacity. As a result, several logging companies on Vancouver Island operate triple-trailer combinations over their own private road system and, in Montana, it is claimed that one Peterbilt tractor hauled six full pup trailers regularly over a road network that presumably did not have many steep gradients. Gross weights of 300 tonnes are often realised on these hauls.

Coping with extra long tree lengths might present few problems on private roads but, on regular highways, it is a different matter. In the UK and Europe, such a situation is unlikely to arise, but in western parts of the USA, logging companies are frequently faced with the task of hauling one huge log from the forest to a distant mill which has customers requiring specific cut lengths.

One solution has been to employ a 'tag' logger, a novel system employing a regular truck-pole hook-up on to which a second trailer (with its own bunk) is coupled *via* a fifth wheel. The system sounds (and is) fairly complicated but, although complex and costly, it does allow extra long logs to be hauled legally. In Europe, such a vehicle would simply not be allowed to operate whereas, in North America, the attitude is more realistic, legislators recognising that special problems require special attention. As always, manufacturers have been quick to respond to the needs of operators and to provide versatile equipment designed to meet a whole range of operational criteria.

Whole industries have been built up around the log truck business, with companies such as Peerless Page Industries (who use the roadrunner bird as their logo) building custom-built headache racks (incorporating large water tanks for cooling brakes), tag-trailers and self-loading trailers, in addition to a seemingly endless list of special-purpose logging equipment. Rubber-bushed suspension components offering low maintenance are built into all Peerless trailers.

Front overhang is not a problem on the private logging roads of Canada's huge woodland regions. The Pacific P16 is built specifically for the logging industry.

In the UK and Europe, logging vehicles in the true sense are virtually unknown, vehicles engaged on the transportation of timber being straightforward road vehicles designed to accommodate regular sizes and weights.

Another very fundamental difference is that European timber carriers invariably come equipped with a crane capable of doing the loading and unloading. On rigid vehicles, this is normally mounted at the rear of the body while on tractor-trailer combinations it can be mid-mounted. In some instances the crane may be mounted on to the tractor chassis itself, thereby leaving the trailer free of any restriction. This method of mounting on a two-axle tractor usually means that the fifth wheel is in a negative position behind the drive axle, which causes problems in terms of hand-ling, axle loadings and overall length if the unit is coupled to a 12-m (39 ft 4 in) semi-trailer.

Staying legal, especially where axle loadings are concerned, is a problem for all truck operators, but in few instances is this as difficult as for the timber carrier. For one thing, loads are usually taken aboard way off the main road network, far from any weigh scale, and this in itself makes things difficult. Equally problematical is the task of judging the weight of timber, since few woods are of the same density and this can vary anyway depending on the water content.

In view of these difficulties, it is not surprising that many log-truck operators around the world are now using axle-load weighing devices on their vehicles. These come in various guises, but most use some sort of pressure pad designed to measure spring deflection and this information is relayed to the cab where it is displayed as an electronic read-out. As electronic gadgetry becomes more accurate and reliable, it seems likely that similar devices will be found as standard equipment on all types of commercial vehicle in years to come.

INTERNATIONAL CONNECTIONS

In the early days of commercial-vehicle development, certain European truck builders were successful in selling their designs on the US market, but this was soon to be reversed many times over once the American automotive giants got into their stride. So it is rather refreshing to see that, in comparatively recent years, the trend is changing once again, with European truck builders selling their wares into the heartlands of North America.

The formative years of the world's motor industry saw some of the pioneer vehicle builders from mainland Europe seeking to market their products in the USA in various ways. In some instances, they sold the trucks direct, while others marketed their products through an agent who promptly placed a new name on the vehicle. This practice was carried on in many markets over very many years and, even today, trucks bear a name which suits the local market and is not necessarily the name of the builder. Possibly the best known of the imports to North America, so far as trucks were concerned, was that of the Swiss Saurer concern, whose first-class products were to be the precursor of that much revered Mack range of heavies.

World War 1 marked the beginning of the flood of US-built trucks for use in Europe and it was the stalwart service given by the thousands of USA, Liberty, FWD, Jeffery, Nash, Pierce-Arrow, Locomobile and, of course, Mack in the hands of the military, which established a sound foundation for the market. The resultant surplus at the end of hostilities did little to benefit the homespun European truck builders but it did introduce motor trucks to very many people and thus created a firm basis for the benefit of imported US trucks in the years to come.

The 20 years or so after 1918 saw the penetration of the European market by numerous US automakers. Some of the trucks were the result of the reputations gained earlier, while many others were merely the result of American companies setting up production or assembly plants in Europe. Ford moved into France and Denmark very early on, opening up plants in the Netherlands and Germany later; the other US volume-producer, General Motors (GM), followed closely and other marques sold as and when they could. Dodge became established in the UK eventually, losing its American ties, while in other instances European home industries were bought out and US models introduced, such as Vauxhall becoming Chevrolet and Opel being absorbed into GM.

The whole process of bringing in US military trucks to Europe was to repeat itself in the early 1940s, although in much greater numbers, luckily. Again, at the end of hostilities, there was an enormous amount of surplus equipment left behind in Europe and there followed yet another period of accolades for the wartime trucks, which still performed well long after memories of the war had faded. But the difference was in the pattern of replacements, for although the European-based US builders were soon back in production there was no great swing towards American equipment. There were certainly some variations in the trend, of course, with some of the heavier and more expensive US trucks finding peacetime buyers. Unfortunately, the pattern and severity of import duties and quotas blur market trends which would perhaps show different results if technical quality and actual price were allowed to hold sway in the marketplace.

For all that, the big change has been in the emergence of a concerted effort by several major European manufacturers to enter the vast North American market in a sizeable way. Before this could come about, a lot of hard thinking had to be done. North America is a hard nut to crack. Canada is moderately different in that it was part of the old British Empire, later Commonwealth, with all that signified in the enhancement of the chances of British companies achieving export markets there. However, that situation has changed a lot in recent years and there are no easy pickings there any more. Canadians don't see the need to import what they can produce themselves, although the proximity of the USA means that a lot of the trucks have American parentage.

The history of isolationism in the USA proper is well known. The Americans have been producing thousands upon thousands of suitable trucks for industry ever since the motor vehicle shook off the horseless carriage label, so why should people look elsewhere for good trucks? With its background of multi-national human stock for the brainpower and its vast natural resources for energy and materials, let alone its financial strength, who could doubt its powerful position in the market?

As we all know to our cost, nothing stays the same for very long in this world and, with the motor industry being so integrated in the economy of today's industrialised nations, the export trade is of the utmost importance.

It was inevitable that the Swedes would get into North America, but the question was how and when. It might seem simple to put a few trucks into a new market at keen prices and see them take to the road in a blaze of publicity, but it is expensive to ship assembled trucks over 3,000 miles (5,000 km) and make a profit, and that is without setting up all the spare parts and servicing back-up so necessary to maintain anything like a good reputation, especially in a country that has ample manufacturing capacity in the first place.

The sums involved in building quality trucks at a remote location and shipping them over such long distances erode most of the expected profit margin. In addition to this, there is the constant worry in today's volatile world of finance that, by the time the trucks arrive at their destination, the exchange rates will have varied to such an alarming degree that any chance of profit will have flown out of the window.

Volvo recognised all the pitfalls but were willing to try the market, realising the vast potential that the USA offered. Modern business requires that the situation is reviewed constantly, for to miss out on a vast market could mean a competitor coming along and removing any chance of expansion. The first moves came in 1975, when market surveys revealed a possible niche for the F85 in the Class 6 sector for trucks up to 26,000 lb (11.8 tonnes). At around the same time, Daimler-Benz were trying the water with their 1111 and 1113 models.

The key to success lay in not only providing the market with a quality truck at the right price for both builder and user, but also establishing a dealer and distribution network to back up the sales effort.

The acquisition of a long-established name in the US truck market (the White name goes back as far as 1901) and the continuing facilities to produce genuine US truck designs, gave Volvo a unique opportunity to study the design, engineering and customer preferences at the heavy end of the market. By this provision, there was no need to jump in with both feet, but instead they could look critically at what they had acquired and little by little instil a subtle blend of Swedish expertise and American experience.

The first noticeable difference in the Volvo-White stable was that the hood of the conventional models was tapered more acutely at the front end by narrowing as well as dropping the top line in a slope. Both the conventionals and the cabovers were also treated to a dash of Volvo identity – quite literally by the oblique line across the grille.

So now the production facility at Greensboro, North Carolina, turns out F6, F7 and N series trucks alongside the White models, while over towards the west coast at Ogden, Utah, the Autocars which have been part of the White set-up since their acquisition in 1953, make up another division of the Corporation. The Autocar badge has graced header tanks since 1908, although for very many years in the early part of their history they produced only cabovers so the header tank was hidden! In later years, under White control, the marque was mainly reserved for the more

The post-war boom in trans-continental hauling was the direct result of the introduction of specially constructed roll-on/roll-off ferries, especially those linking the UK and the near European continent.

special applications for heavy industry rather than the more typical interstate eighteen-wheelers.

Another recent story of the cross-Atlantic-Ocean drift concerning the world of trucks relates to an old established but ailing truck builder of the UK and that of an equally well known and respected manufacturer from the USA.

In the UK, the friendly rivals of Sandbach in Cheshire – ERF and Foden – were regarded by many enthusiasts as the epitome of British truck building

right up to the 1970s. Historically, ERF was born out of Foden way back in 1933, when family decisions about the future of the original company caused a split. Since that time, the products of both marques have earned tremendous reputations for reliability, with many fleets lining up behind one or other of the two.

The violent downturn in markets for heavy trucks was having serious consequences for most of the worlds' truck builders in the period of the late 1970s and both these respected names were said to be in real

The Hino marque in Ireland covered a wide selection of vehicles, from delivery vans right up to maximum capacity eight-wheelers.

trouble. A merger of the two famous names was bandied about by some, but it had no foundation. As time went on, the agony increased, with rumours of possible closure of Foden with all that entailed for the fast-shrinking British heavy-truck industry.

Then came the news: Foden acquired by Paccar. Some saw it as the salvation and possible expansion of a company that, over the years, had created an aura all its own whenever the topic of best trucks was discussed. For Foden was revered amongst the lorry fraternity (or we should really say 'wagons', for that is the phrase used in the north of England where much heavy transport has been produced). The news that the name was to continue, albeit in revived form, was met with a sigh of relief, if not rapturous applause.

For the real diehards, who saw in Foden the embodiment of all that was 'British and best', the news was catastrophic. How on earth could the Yanks get involved in building Fodens? They might be okay at building lumbering long-wheelbase tractors, with all those chrome exhaust stacks, fancy paint-jobs, and deep-buttoned plush sleeper pods, but it was sacrilege to let them loose with something so Britannic as the heritage of Fodens.

Well, as the past few years bear witness, it has worked, this unlikely marriage of British experience and American technology. By thorough appraisal, careful evaluation and precise manipulation, the latest Fodens are earning new reputations and confounding the critics. One striking element of this success was through the introduction of new gross weights in the UK in 1983, when all the pundits were airing their views as to the optimum way of handling the revised gross for artics of 38 tonnes. Should the new outfits be 2 + 3 or 3 + 2 layout, referring to axles on tractor and semi. Then it was whether the tractors should be twin-steered or rear-steer, should they have lift axles, tag axles, single tyres or twins, steel springs or air suspension.

Only then did Fodens make their move, and what was it to be – a 6 × 4 no less! With little fuss, they announced that some operators might prefer the extra stability and reduced risk of overloading that comes with operating a 6 × 4 and, oh yes, it weighed a little over 7 tonnes.

American influence has been gradual but firm. The original new title of Sandbach Engineering was replaced in 1984 by the more familiar sounding Foden Trucks and the outward appearance was not a million miles different from what it might have possibly been under the old regime. It is under the skin that the Kenworth model has developed, with the accent on weight saving and attendant fuel economy as befits a truck of these hard times. Even the advertising has taken on the Paccar mantle with the emphasis on quality and 'class'. Whereas the 6 × 4 has been historically a heavy-haulage configuration, and that also means heavy in unladen weight and fuel consumption, Fodens have gone to great lengths to point out the meagre increase in weight of their tractor over a 4 × 2. By the use of light alloy in wheels, air reservoirs, fuel tanks and parts of the drive axles, together with torsion-bar suspension taken from Kenworth designs, the weight is not that much different from some 6 × 2 rear-steer-layout tractors.

Now, to turn to the other part of the Foden family in truck building, we find that its name was to be linked to quite a well-known name from much further afield than the USA. As something of a prelude to that, we need to go back just a little earlier to that period of motor-industry history when home sales were falling in the face of intense foreign competition.

Having seen the decimation of the British motorcycle industry by the high-revving Japanese models, and then the erosion of the largely home-produced private-car market, it was no wonder that some people got decidedly hot under the collar at the sight of a few Hino trucks on the British scene in the late 1970s. There were reports of strong-feeling pro-British workers refusing to handle any loads carried on Japanese heavy trucks and stories of a banning of such vehicles from any British Leyland plants.

This little fracas had its origins in Ireland where, with virtually no home industry of its own, some motor assemblers began putting together Hinos for use in Ireland. Now the Republic of Ireland does not have a long history of vehicle building, although there has been car production on a small scale, plus the Ford works at Cork. Independent builders of trucks have occurred, with the assembly in the mid-

1930s of the Beardmore Multiwheeler hybrid artic and then assembly of Volvos in Dublin at about the same time.

In post-war years, plans were laid to build a truck-manufacturing or assembly facility in collaboration with Leyland and the plant was actually about ready for production, with machinery installed, when a change of government reversed the decision.

So the assembly of trucks had to wait about another 20 years for anything new to transpire and this time it was left to free enterprise, in the shape of Harris Assemblers of Dublin, to get the show on the road. It was not long before the previous truck builders who had done so well in Eire for many years began to feel the pinch. Historically, it had been British trucks which had sold well in the Emerald Isle so it was firms like Commer, Leyland, Ford, Austin and Bedford who lost orders to the newly assembled foreigner.

Flushed with its success at home, Harris looked further afield for additions to its market and naturally decided that the British mainland was ripe for attention, particularly in view of the gradual decline of Leyland sales at the hands of importers supplying products from Sweden, the Netherlands and Germany. A handful of Hinos were soon at work for British operators, where the market seemed willing to try anything so long as the price was right. This was during the period when British Leyland was taking a knocking from all quarters: operators, users, drivers and, of course, the press.

But the expected, nay feared, swamping of the British truck scene just did not happen. True there were a few to be seen around, and some fleets did include several, but the acid test of everyday hard work soon proved that the Hino was no wonder truck and they did not attract the hordes of buyers that some had envisaged. In the early 1980s, one could spend a day on the motorways of the country and the number of Hinos seen might amount to three or four and some of these might be Irish-registered. One particular area might have more than another but then these would be tippers engaged on local work and not usually seen on long distance runs.

So it seemed like a bolt from the blue, when, in 1982, news broke that ERF, the only remaining independent British truck builder, was looking at the possibility of buying certain Hino parts to help with the projected new 12/15-tonner. But it was firmly denied that Hinos would be brought into the UK directly by ERF, or that any new ERF might really be a badge-engineered Hino.

By the time the 50-year celebrations were under way at ERF, there was plenty of speculation concerning the joint ERF/Hino deal which was under discussion. This was in relation to a range of four-wheel 12- to 15-tonne chassis using a variety of Hino parts, including the steel cab. It was planned to use the Perkins 6.354 engine with Hino gearbox and axles. By September, there was talk of a pilot model being assembled at the ERF Sandbach works, close by the new M16 models, and then, at the end of the year, ERF announced that the project had been delayed because of technical and commercial reasons, with no date being mentioned of a possible introduction. So the half-century year for ERF had certainly been one of major decisions. There had been much agonising since 1980 when both the Cheshire-based truck builders – ERF and Foden – had faced similar problems of falling sales and mounting costs. There was even talk that the two rivals might join forces in order to weather the storm, but neither was in very good shape. The usual medicine of shedding sections of the work force, reducing stocks and cutting costs were put into action and, somehow, ERF managed to weather the storm while its close relation and neighbour suffered a takeover.

So ERF was at least spared that ignominity and was able to get to the post in 1983, although it had become decidedly leaner on the way. Fifty years of continuous lorry production is no mean feat for such a modest company, although, as they are quick to point out, at least in 1983 they built more heavy-weights than Foden or Seddon-Atkinson. Note that we speak of *lorry* production for, like so many other British builders, that was the term for the commercial vehicles of the day; the term 'truck' was reserved for those little American runabouts with the high-revving petrol engines. For many years, the byline on ERF advertisements read 'builders of the world's finest oil-engined lorries'.

At the same time as Hino sales were going so well in Ireland, a local trailer builder decided that the market could well support a truly individual Irish-built truck to rival the constant stream of imported Volvo, Nissan and Fiat. The Dennison brothers set-up was to manufacture the chassis frames themselves from sections bought in. Naturally, the larger running units were of reputable make in order to provide a reliable and saleable vehicle, while other smaller items were either built up by Dennison themselves or obtained from local suppliers.

The first truck was put on the road in 1977 and, in the $3\frac{1}{2}$ years of production, some 250 vehicles were produced and sold but, like so many other engineering-based industries, the recession of the early 1980s took its toll and Dennison ceased to build trucks.

Because of the close proximity of the British mainland, it was natural that the UK market was looked at for the hoped-for breakthrough into exports. Unfortunately for Dennison, their plans could not have come at a worse time, for there were huge stocks of unsold trucks lying about in the UK, with home producers and importers suffering alike. With such a large Irish population in the UK, it was hoped that the trucks could have found buyers who would have supported their old home country and, to be sure, a few Dennisons found their way into the waste-disposal fleets in north London, these being rigid eight-wheelers. The tractor model also found a few buyers in the UK, with one user actually going to great lengths to secure additions to his fleet, after production had ceased, with the intention of having an all-Dennison fleet.

SHIPS OF THE DESERT

The desert is tranquil. Mile after endless undulating mile of wind-swept sand bakes beneath the heat of a searing sun. No hint of life exists in this barren yet beautiful land but, below its shifting surface, lies 'crude', the black liquid gold which plays such a vital part in our world's economy.

And where there's oil, there are trucks. For the oil men there is little tranquillity. The natural beauty of the land is overlooked. The environment in which they live and work is a hostile, lonely region seemingly designed to present as many problems as possible to the functions of driving and maintaining vehicles and it is this attitude which is nearer the truth. To those of us with a touch of Lawrence of Arabia in our blood, the isolation of the desert has a million

Quite at home on a sea of shifting sand, these huge Kenworth 953 ships of the desert are used to haul oilfield drilling equipment from one well site to the next. Contrary to common belief, deserts are rarely flat and Bedouin drivers are often employed in order that the best possible passage across the sand is followed.

attractions but the reality is less appealing and those who live there, and who work on oilfield exploration or support vehicles, do so for money, not love.

Oilfield trucks, like the men who work with them, are a special breed. Over the years, many manufacturers have attempted to build vehicles capable of withstanding the strain of overloading, overheating and the abrasive qualities of sand – and most have failed. Today only a few purpose-built desert trucks are made, these coming mainly from Kenworth, Oshkosh, MOL and Iveco but the unequalled master of them all is the KW 953, the huge 6 × 6 truck beloved of every Bedouin driver and respected by Arab and oil-company executive alike.

Kenworth's 953 is a real desert rig designed specifically to haul super-heavy loads over almost impassable terrain. It is big, standard models standing over 14 ft (4.26 m) tall and stretching 40 ft (12 m) in overall length. Twin vertical exhausts, located one each side of the long narrow hood, point skyward like Bofors guns and one only has to catch a fleeting sound of a 953 in full song to instantly recognise the high pitched scream of a 12V-71N Detroit.

Many hazards face the driver of a desert truck and the more obvious of these include soft, drifted sand and ground clearance. The 953 combats these problems by using a combination of giant 21.00 × 25 'Sand Tread' tyres and all-wheel drive. In this way, maximum ground clearance is achieved and the weight transferred by the flotation tyres is kept to an absolute minimum. Hub-reduction Clark axles front and rear help take the strain imposed by driveline shock and Kenworth's tough 38.5-short ton (35-tonne) capacity walking-beam suspension provides maximum articulation for the rear bogie.

But the most distinctive feature of the 953 is its twin radiator arrangement at the front end, which gives the impression of the bow of a ship rather than the hood of a truck. This feature is not cosmetic, however, and by using two cooling radiators, engine overheating problems are greatly reduced. KW engineers probably don't approve of the practice, but another method of keeping things cool is to remove all the thermostats in the cooling system for times when things are really warming up.

A variety of tasks befalls the desert truck and its drivers and these include moving drilling rigs, either whole or in parts, from one site to another and relocating the living accommodation. These jobs may not sound difficult, until one remembers that roads don't exist and, contrary to common belief, deserts are not flat. In fact, grades of 30% are sometimes negotiated by oilfield trucks and one of the most impressive sights in the world is that of a rig being moved by a team of Kenworths, two of which support the wide base, while the third carries the narrower top. This method saves valuable time since the rig does not have to be broken down and later re-assembled. It also means that the Kenworth at the back of the convoy has to negotiate the whole journey in reverse since the tip of the rig is supported on the body of the truck. The skill of the Bedouin drivers is unparalleled and to witness such a move, and hear the exquisitely timed gearshifts of the two leading rigs and wonder at the reversing ability of the rearmost, is akin to seeing one of the seven wonders of the world.

Oilfield trucks are normally fitted with large, rugged platform bodies known as 'floats' and these feature a steel roller at the extreme rear end, which is designed to assist in winching rigs and other heavy loads up on to the truck. Winches are an essential part of any oilfield truck but the method of loading means that enormous stresses are imposed on the rear of the frame and the truck's rear suspension. When heavy loads are winched aboard, this results in the rear of the truck being pulled towards the ground with the inevitable result that the nose points towards the sky! Incredibly, trucks used in the desert are designed to accept this sort of punishment as part of the everyday routine, so there is little risk of the components failing.

Without doubt, the huge, impressive trucks used to haul the actual rigs and ancillary gear across the world's oilfields are the most interesting to the truck lover. But many other vehicles are also employed in the search for crude. Schlumberger, an international organisation specialising in the analysis of data obtained by lowering seeker probes into the ground, operates a fleet of International and Kenworth trucks, each of which contains equipment worth over $1 million. These vehicles are used not only to determine the

W inching huge loads up over the rear of the oilfield 'float' body imposes tremendous strains on the chassis and rear suspension, but oilfield trucks such as this Kenworth 953 take such punishment in their stride.

most likely spots to drill, but also to provide up-to-date information on how drilling activities are progressing. The equipment carried inside the shell-like bodywork includes a giant winch carrying miles of cable and a host of computer terminals designed to decode the information received by the seeker probes lowered into the ground.

Other oilfield 'support' trucks include 'well stimulator' vehicles such as those operated by Canadian Tracmaster. These trucks, normally 8 × 4 long-wheelbase Kenworths, carry auxiliary engines and compressors to drilling sites and are then used to pump slurry down into the ground under pressure, in the hope that this will displace the oil and send it to the surface. Although not the most interesting trucks in appearance, this type of vehicle nevertheless performs an essential role in the oil-exploration industry.

Oil is big business and, as may be expected, every vehicle used in its discovery and extraction represents a hefty financial investment. Interestingly, some of the biggest and most extravagant trucks used in the deserts of the Middle East are not connected with oilfields in any way, unless of course one draws a line between the value of oil itself and the wealth of the owners. Amazingly, oil-rich sheiks have purchased Mercedes and Kenworth desert-spec vehicles not to look for oil, but to tour the desert on hunting expeditions. Falconry is a favourite sport among the wealthiest sheiks and in an exercise, without financial constraints, to see who can design and build the most luxurious and ostentatious mobile palaces, some incredible vehicles have emerged. A typical example boasts living space for twelve persons, bathrooms with solid gold fittings, fully equipped kitchen and bedrooms, all complete with air conditioning and piped music! No doubt, someone, somewhere, is already attempting to find a way of including a swimming pool in the specification! But whatever the reasons, it is true to say that even the private trucks found in the desert cost over £1 million!

THE HEAVY GANG

Travel by road in virtually any part of the world and you will see heavy haulage in action. Bouncing along a half-hidden track in the Brazilian forests will be a Scania 6 × 4 bonneted tractor, hauling a tracked excavator on a low-loader semi-trailer. The roar of the engine will be amplified by the dense undergrowth as the heavily laden vehicle rumbles by to disappear from view around a bend. Or turn a corner in a picturesque Bavarian town and you may be brought to a halt by a parked police car, its warning beacons signalling that something special is on the move. Behind it, crossing your line of vision, a 20-axle Goldhofer modular bogie – complete with Titan tractors front and rear – moves slowly as it transports the mammoth 300-tonne transformer to the nearby power station.

The monotony of the sun-drenched Australian outback will be broken on occasion by the awesome bulk of a Wabco dump-truck which completely dwarfs the extending-width Drake trailer on which it is being

Despite the difficulties presented by narrow roads and steep hills, a great deal of heavy, specialised haulage takes place in tiny Switzerland. Knecht operate this smart push/pull combination with Magirus-Deutz motive power seen here at the Brown-Boveri plant in Baden.

hauled. At the business end, a Cummins 450-hp diesel provides the power for the 6×4 Kenworth K100 belonging to Bell Bros as the rig sets out on the long haul from Sydney to Western Australia. At something over 2,000 miles (3,200 km), this is one of the longest heavy haulage moves on earth.

Naturally, it is the really gigantic loads which tend to attract the most attention when on the move, but by far the greatest numbers of loads which are oversized or overweight are moved by 6×4 'dual purpose' tractors.

These 'maids-of-all-work' operate with a wide range of semi-trailers and are, in themselves, similar in appearance to 6×4 units used in more conventional highway-haulage roles. They are used to move long, self-supporting loads, such as bridge beams, using a bolster attachment temporarily fixed to the fifth wheel. At the rear end, the load rides on two, three or even four axles, which combine to make a

'dolly'. These are often home-built by the operator who has rigged up an old chassis with spare axle components.

Types of trailers in use encompass an encyclopaedia of designs, including basic low-loaders (with as many as four self-steering axles) or the European-favoured extendable dropframe designs with as many as six axles, four of which can be self-tracking. Outside Europe, very rugged heavy-duty low-loaders with 'jeep' dollies are popular. Semi-trailers derived from the modular bogie concept are being used in increasing numbers in many countries and, as with the pure modular principle, extra components providing additional capacity can be added if necessary.

P eterbilt with jeep-divider/dolly and low-bed trailer leaves construction site with a truly massive bulldozer as load.

Using well-proven basic units by such manufacturers as Daimler-Benz and ZF, the Titan heavy-haulage tractor models have shown up well against the more old-established builders. This Dutch example of the eight-wheel unit is in articulated form.

Tractor units used in this category, whether forward control or bonneted, are mostly 6 × 4 in configuration, although a few beefier 6 × 6 models are also used. Generally speaking, power is in the 330-hp to 400-hp bracket, depending on the area of operation. The trucks themselves are normally 'heavy-duty' versions derived from the standard production-line range produced by individual manufacturers. Apart from having larger, more powerful engines, heavier transmissions are fitted and the option of a torque-converter is now appearing on many manufacturers' lists of 'special' options. Axles with higher ratings than usual and fifth wheel couplings with double the 'normal' capacity will also form part of the package that, when finally unwrapped, reveals a vehicle capable of playing many parts on the general and specialised road-transport scene.

Built to comply with the legislation controlling the country or countries in which they will be operated, these vehicles will use many other non-driveline components common to other models from the same stable. This standardisation of parts enables a heavy-weight tractor to be produced at an acceptable cost, while taking into account the specialised and individual requirements of each operator. Flexibility is the name of the game in this particular weight category.

Throughout Europe and Scandinavia, while regulations might vary slightly from country to country, the majority of road-haulage vehicles are built to approximately the same dimensions. True, overall lengths and axle loadings are sometimes different, but most European trucks at least conform to a 2.5-m (8 ft 2½ in) width limit.

It is obviously desirable to build, and operate, machines which are multi-functional and acceptable to a wide variety of operators. Tractors capable of performing more than one job are capable of blending in

with fast-flowing traffic and this ability to keep up the same pace as lighter vehicles is a bonus. It is for this reason that many so called 'heavy-haulage' tractors only become evident to the majority of road users when travelling in a heavily laden condition and with a full complement of escort vehicles, including police cars with flashing beacons and pilot vans displaying warning notices such as 'Bred Last', 'Schwertransport', 'Convoi Exceptionnel', 'Transporti Eccezionali' etc, depending upon the country of operation.

Most operations are carried out in various types of articulated configuration with the few nonconformers resorting to some kind of ballast weight, often nothing more than a few hefty concrete blocks chained to the fifth wheel coupling. A small number of operators in this weight class do use proper, custom-built ballast boxes which can be easily lifted on or off the chassis by crane or forklift. But these are in a minority for the obvious reason of cost.

There is no clearly defined point at which heavy-haulage tractors used exclusively for the really heavy hauls take over from the type of vehicles described above. Indeed modern manufacturing and engineering facilities now make it possible to incorporate into those vehicles many of the features and capabilities which have for many years been available only in larger and generally heavier designs. But without doubt, Europe and the UK have always been recog-

The requirement for a large cab capable of accommodating the crew of a heavy-haulage tractor is often overlooked but those companies using Tatra 813 tractors are always assured of adequate crew space. Here a pair of boilers on German Scheuerle modules are hauled by Tatra 813 8 × 8 tractors. Power is provided by a 19-litre V12 diesel. Czech state-controlled company CSAD is the specialist company involved in this haul.

nised as the home of the pure-bred, purpose-built, drawbar tractor unit.

The history of these vehicles can be traced back to the early days of steam traction, when all loads were drawn or hauled by hissing, steaming machines. These were eventually replaced by the diesel engine and the instant power offered by this new concept was immediately welcomed by the road transport fraternity.

Following World War 2 and the dramatic development of European manufacturing and engineering techniques, exports increased rapidly and manufacturers of heavy-haulage tractors began to produce vehicles for use outside of their own domestic market. Many of these were despatched to 'backward' underdeveloped nations, but still retained the basic elements of European philosophy inherent in their original design. At the same time, on the opposite side of the Atlantic, developments in heavy haulage had taken a rather different direction.

Still in use behind the Iron Curtain are three Scammell Contractors exported to the USSR in the early 1970s. Units were sold complete with purpose-built ballast boxes and matched 300-tonne capacity Crane Fruehauf trailer. Load here is a 190-tonne transformer.

Illustrating perfectly the American preference for fifth wheel hook-ups is this rare Hendrickson 8 × 4 tractor hauling a 220-tonne transformer in New York state. The tractor was one of a specially-built pair ordered for Higgins Erectors and featured a V12 producing 600 hp. Rear suspension was a 150-tonne walking beam, Hendrickson naturally!

American operators, and therefore the manufacturers, adopted the attitude that ballasted vehicles were not suitable for their operations. Instead they preferred to use large articulated tractors with a divider dolly or 'jeep' interposed between the tractor and semi-trailer.

The 'jeep' is basically a one-, two- or tri-axle dolly, rugged in construction but with non-steering axles and designed to couple into a fifth wheel by means of a normal kingpin. Atop the jeep is another fifth wheel coupling into which the trailer kingpin is located.

By using this system, up to 25% of the load (and weight of the semi-trailer) can be transferred to the tractor's driven axles, thereby ensuring traction under all but the most extreme circumstances. In really difficult conditions, it was not unknown for operators to place ballast blocks on the neck of the jeep itself to assist with traction.

Because of the wider roads on which these vehicles were driven, equipment of this type was rather larger than that used by European operators to move the same-sized load. However, in the strictest terms,

direct comparisons between the two different systems are not easy. Suffice it to say that the North American jeep dividers were simple, robust and often fabricated by innovative truckers who indulged themselves in an orgy of over-engineering. Trailers too were often built from steel girders, with a few axles hung on as required. Steering mechanisms were largely unknown, operators preferring to keep things as simple as possible. In the few instances where steering systems were attempted, these were confined to straightforward power rams operated by a trailer steersman in cases of emergency.

It was not until the early 1970s that European 'modular' trailer systems began to appear on the roads of the USA and Canada. Today, however, every manufacturer of this type of equipment is represented by a dealer or distributor throughout the North American continent.

It was the introduction of these sophisticated trailers that resulted in the gradual decline of the jeep/dolly principle, especially with really heavy loads. In their place have appeared massive hydraulic

gooseneck assemblies which, at times, dwarf the tractor unit and are coupled to modular bogies having anything up to twenty axle lines per trailer.

Although wide use was made of heavy-duty tractor units available from the numerous American truck builders, the heavy-haulage industry on that continent has also enjoyed a long tradition of modifying or completely rebuilding equipment in order to tailor-make a specialised heavy-haulage unit. Massive construction equipment with equally huge power offered tremendous possibilities for purpose-built tractors and many such conversions were undertaken.

One such design which proved ideal for hauling really heavy weights such as those often encountered in the nuclear power programme, was the Mack M75 SX, a 6 × 6 off-highway dump-truck rated conservatively at 75 short tons (68 tonnes) payload. This machine, which stood an intimidating 13 ft (4 m) in

Not immediately recognisable, thanks to cab modifications, is this 500-hp Faun tractor used in Sweden by Vattenfall Heavy Haulage. Load is a turbine shaft which is loaded aboard a Nicolas bogie. Powerful 6 × 6 tractor features massive winch and snow chains. Cab modification allow units to be loaded on to rail wagons for returning to base when empty.

width and which measured 28 ft (8.5 m) in overall length, without the dump bowl overhang, quickly gained popularity with several operators in its new role as a heavy-haulage tractor. A Cummins V12 developing no less than 800 hp was available in this chassis and the Clark torque-converter and eight-speed transmission also proved acceptable for the task at hand. In essence, it was simply a question of removing the dump bowl and tipping gear and substituting a fifth wheel assembly. So popular was this unit to become with heavy haulers that, for a while, Mack

V̲ast re-heater vessel weighing over 400 tons is seen *en route* from Larne in Northern Ireland to Belfast. The push/pull outfit comprises two of Wrekin Roadways Contractors and Cometto bogies. Vessel was shipped to San Onofre, California, where it was unloaded onto Lampson crawler tracks for its final leg of the epic journey.

marketed the chassis only, thereby saving those intent on conversions the trouble and expense of removing the body.

One such Mack M75 was converted by Hoffman International and, when fitted with a fifth wheel, boasted an almost unbelievable capacity of 1,000 short tons (907 tonnes)! This unit was used by Hoffman on several contracts for the nuclear power programme and regularly hauled loads approaching 800 short tons (726 tonnes). These were carried on a specially designed Talbert trailer which employed the 'Schnable' principle. In this format, the trailer consisted of two massive goosenecks, each with its own running gear. For moving reactor pressure vessels (RPV), the goosenecks were clamped to each end of the load, making it an integral part of the trailer.

Other notable rebuilds of the same period included conversions to Mack vehicles carried out by Reliance Truck. Again these started life as Mack dump-trucks, but were re-engineered by the operator and converted into tractor units complete with a second steering axle. Contrary to trends in transatlantic heavy haulage at that time, these unusual vehicles often operated with purpose-built ballast-box bodies which were even painted in the operator's fleet colours. They also enjoyed the distinction of operating with the first self-steering, hydraulically-levelling Nicolas bogies in North America. These French-built units represented the first of their type to enter service with a major heavy hauler and their impact on American users was dramatic.

The idea of 500 short tons (454 tonnes) on a semi-trailer seems unlikely at best, yet it happened! Frank

Headed up by a chain-driven Pacific M26 tractor and pushed by a Fiat 6 × 4 is this 250-ton stator loaded aboard the Cometto trailer employing the Schnable principle. This means that the load is self-supporting, being connected to the trailer at each end. Italian operator Fumigali is the specialist involved here.

Hake, a specialised heavy hauler from Philadelphia, had just such a monster which was moved around by two, or even three, rebuilt Euclid dump-trucks. These had started life as normal dumpers, but were converted in the Hake workshop to twin-steer tractors equipped with two engines located side by side!

The normal method of operation was for one tractor to hook up to the front of the trailer whilst, at the rear, there was room for two to operate alongside each other and push whenever required. Because of its massive size, however, the trailer was not easily moved over long distances and, whenever this was necessary, it was stripped down and the separate components shipped by rail.

With non-steering axles, negotiating a tight corner was difficult with a heavy load aboard. This problem was overcome by placing steel plates on the road at the appropriate point and making these slippery by adding generous amounts of grease. Simple! The trailer and load were then winched sideways on the greased steel by one of the tractors. Hardly sophisticated, but practical in the true North American tradition. So, while the Europeans favoured the idea of a purpose-built drawbar machine, the North Americans remained wedded firmly to the fifth wheel.

Because of similarities in operating conditions in many overseas markets, the jeep/dolly system has been widely adopted by many countries outside of its native USA. Australia and South Africa are prime examples, both having large numbers of American heavy trucks active in their heavy-haulage industry. European modular trailers began to appear in South Africa at the same time as they were entering the American market, although their introduction to

Australian operators has been more recent. However, today, the modular concept is well established in both Australia and South Africa.

Keeping their options open, most Australian companies using this type of trailer have been using tractors with concrete blocks as ballast. Purpose-built ballast boxes are rare, although a few operators, including Lance Smith and Walter J. Wright, do use them on certain chassis. In South Africa, too, the huge Omnibus Transport Group once used a trio of carefully specified Kenworth Brute tractors, each of which featured its own matching ballast-box body.

Meanwhile, back in Europe, operators engaged in specialised heavy hauling could choose from an incredibly wide range of specialised motive units which included configurations such as 4 × 4, 6 × 4, 6 × 6, 8 × 6, 8 × 8 or even 10 × 8. Not many years ago, the majority of these machines would have been supplied as ballasted units only. Today, in most instances, they are available as fifth-wheel tractors, too, but with detachable ballast bodies of course. Vehicles of this type are built by Faun, Kaelble, MAN, Mercedes and Titan, all of which are German manufacturers. Others offer-

ing similar vehicles include FTF and Terberg from the Netherlands, the Belgian MOL, French Renault and Iveco, the latter hailing from both Italy and Germany. Last, but by no means least, is the Scammell, a name most will recognise as being thoroughly British.

Mercedes and Iveco favour their own 'in-house' power plants while the other manufacturers use proprietary engines from Cummins, Detroit Diesel, Mercedes and KHD. Power outputs range from a modest 350 hp to a more impressive 800 hp and transmissions in the lower weight ranges tend to be of the manual type, although many have the option of a torque-converter to assist with the tricky business of pulling away from a standing start. Above 150-tonnes gross weight, automatic transmissions are

Mack M75 SX dump-trucks proved so popular with heavy-haulage companies that Mack produced the vehicles without the usual dump bucket in order that modifications could be made to them without the operator first having to throw away the body. The Nicolas trailer with the enormous neck is an early model 3.66 m (12 ft) wide and sold in the USA as the 'heavy duty' model. This was later adopted for use in Europe.

often considered as 'standard' equipment and these too come matched to torque-converters and often incorporate lock-up retarders.

Allison and ZF are chosen by most manufacturers, although Scammell offer Allison only. One of the reasons for this concerns the important consideration of 'standardisation' wherever possible. This is in the interest of everyone since, in the event of a failure, it is imperative that the vehicle is repaired and back in service as quickly as possible and, despite the most

Allis-Chalmers bulldozer, minus its blade, is transported in Australia by an Atkinson L6066C tractor and Drake semi-trailer. Tractor features a Cummins 350 and Omega rear bogie. Drake trailer extends from 2.5 m (8 ft 2 in) in width to a maximum of 4.25 m (14 ft). A divider-dolly is used to distribute the load.

stringent maintenance and regular servicing, breakdowns do happen. Heavy-haulage tractors are not exempt from mechanical failure, despite the care with which the components are selected and assembled. This takes into account the fact that, although heavy-haulage machines are given a 'nominal gross rating' by manufacturers, these ratings are often exceeded when the vehicles are in service.

In drawbar operations, the amount of ballast placed on a tractor unit is not a hit-and-miss affair but something carefully calculated to ensure maximum tractive effort. Attempt to move 400 tonnes on a drawbar with an unballasted tractor at full power and this will inevitably result in the unit's rear bogie attempting to leave the ground. A case of wheel spin par excellence!

The amount of tractive effort, or pulling power, is

directly related to the vehicle's laden weight. A dry road surface will provide far better adhesion than a wet one and this difference could be crucial. Too little ballast and you may lose traction and become stranded. Too much and you are not only carrying around excess weight, but carrying it to no avail. The optimum figure on dry, compacted surfaces is around 70% of the laden tractor's weight.

Tandem rear bogies with capacities of 40 tonnes are commonplace on large tractors and it should be remembered that this rating is nominal. As mentioned earlier, many tractors, even the real heavies, are built to a 2.5-m (8 ft $2\frac{1}{2}$ in) overall width but, with heavier rear axles and larger hub-reduction gearing, overall widths are creeping out and 2.856 m (9 ft 5 in) is now becoming more popular.

Operators and manufacturers work closely together to ensure that the right machine for the job is available when it is required. Generally speaking, this co-operation works well but there are occasions when a frustrated operator, having a specific requirement, is unable to convince the truck (or trailer) builder that they should build a 'one-off' for a particular task. This was the situation that faced an operator called Heinrich Schutz in 1979.

Schutz was looking for a 6 × 6 design of compact size, capable of handling loads up to 200 tonnes and equipped with a 400-bhp engine. Existing manufacturers could not meet his requirements so, in desperation, he approached Titan GmbH. This company had specialised for many years in building crane carriers, dump-trucks, steelworks vehicles and other heavy-duty equipment.

Recognised as the largest heavy haulage tractors in regular road use are the huge Pacific P12W3 6 × 4 units operated by the heavy-haulage division of South African Railways. Powered by 600-hp Cummins diesels, the Pacifics feature a permanent ballast-box-cum-crew quarters behind the cab. Load is a 220-tonne Flash Stage measuring 65 m (213 ft) in length. Trailer is a Nicolas modular outfit. No less than twenty-three Pacifics are operated by SAR.

They accepted the challenge offered by Heinrich Schutz and, working closely together, the combined talents of heavy-haulage operator and specialist manufacturer produced the first Titan tractor. The remarkably effective approach to the problem was to take a production Mercedes 2632 tractor unit and completely rebuild it. The standard engine was replaced by the more powerful OM404–420 hp unit, a ZF torque-converter transmission was fitted and the axles and chassis frame were strengthened for heavy-duty operations.

The new tractors were an immediate success and, whilst initially built for Schutz, were soon made available to other heavy-haulage operators. Today, they can be found in many haulage fleets across Europe and Scandinavia and a number are operating with European contractors in the Middle-Eastern oilfields.

Initially built to 6 × 6 configuration, the Titan is now offered in 8 × 6, 8 × 8 and 10 × 8 models and still based largely on the same original Mercedes design and componentry. To meet desert conditions, Titan built a 6 × 6 tractor, fitted with the turbo-charged version of the OM 404. This engine produces 525 hp and

Of an awkward size rather than weight are these Caterpillar 631 scrapers loaded aboard Hyster semi-trailers in South Africa. Operated by Heavy Transport & Plant Hire, the tractors are 8 × 4 units featuring an unusual tridem rear bogie. Second unit is a South African Ralph, the third unit built by Ralph Lewis.

has since become the standard power unit for the complete range. The most recent model uses a MAN cab and is an 8 × 6 tractor in an unusual rear-steer configuration with the second steering axle being non-driven. The Mercedes V-12 engine installed in this model produces a hefty and useful 625 hp.

Despite the fact that these tractors are purchased and then completely rebuilt, they have the very considerable advantage of being fully covered by the Mercedes warranty worldwide, with all that this implies. Not surprisingly, perhaps, Mercedes themselves have now introduced their own 6 × 6 500-hp tractor unit. Built at the former Saurer plant in Switzerland, the new tractor supplements the long-established Mercedes three-axle tractor range, which is very popular with German operators. Assembled by the proud and precise Saurer craftsmen, the 3850 is al-

ready setting new standards in excellence for this type of truck. Two of these new machines have been purchased by the Abnormal Loads Division of South African Railways, who operate perhaps the largest fleet of pure heavy-haulage equipment in the world. In South Africa, they are operated alongside the massive Pacifics of the Abnormal Loads Division, and also the Mack and Foden tractors. The Foden 6 × 4s feature locally built cabs and 400-hp Caterpillar engines.

Faun in Germany have, for many years, offered what is possibly the largest range of heavy-haulage tractors, from 4 × 4 to 8 × 8 configurations, mostly bonneted designs rather than forward control models.

Two of the largest tractors ever built by Faun were the HZ70/80 8 × 8 units for Iberduero in Spain. There they operated with Trabosa modular trailers, transporting heavyweight loads for the Spanish nuclear power programme. With a nominal gross weight rating of 70 tonnes, the vast bonneted machines were powered by General Motors V-16 diesel engine, developing 800 hp and driving through an Allison torque-converter transmission. 1200–24PR 20 tyre equipment was fitted to the 30-tonne front bogie and the

Finnish heavy-haulage specialist, Imatrans Voima operate this Scheuerle self-propelled transporter which features hydrostatic drive in the hubs of the motive unit. Seen here with a 220-tonne load, the combination makes slow but steady progress in Northern Finland.

40-tonne rear bogie. For the heaviest loads, up to 100 tonnes of ballast could be added to each machine, making the tractors virtually abnormal loads in themselves. Nominally rated at 400-tonnes gtw, each tractor was some 12 m (39 ft 4 in) long, 2.8 (9 ft 2 in) in width and measured an incredible 3.8 m ($12\frac{1}{2}$ ft) to the cab roof.

Kaelble have a long tradition of supplying heavy tractors to the German Federal Railways and their very large 4 × 4 Kaelble bonneted draw-bar tractors were a familiar sight for many years. They have always built a range of 6 × 6 machines for the West German market and export heavy tractors to a variety of other markets, including North Africa. The German Federal Railways (Deutsche Bundesbahn) also operate a Scheuerle self-propelled transporter.

This fascinating piece of equipment is based on a pair of five-axle modular bogies from the Scheuerle range but mounted between them is an extra two-axle set which runs on 10.00 × 20 tyres as opposed to the 7.50 × 15 fitted to the other axles. The two-axle set is hydrostatically powered with motors in each hub, power for the hydrostatic drive pump being provided by a Deutz 304-hp air-cooled engine. A superstructure housing the engine and the driver's compartment is mounted atop one end of the twelve-axle machine and the hydraulic steering and suspension mechanism common throughout the Scheuerle range is retained in the transporter.

Operating as a single unit, the transporter can carry 250 tonnes. The Federal Railways also employ two similar units, which carry a girder-frame bridge

Amongst the very last Super Contractors built were these two Pickfords tractors pictured double-heading a 333-tonne casting. A 250-tonne MAN Jumbo brings up the rear. Hauled on a twenty-four line modular trailer, the load was *en route* from Selby to Sheffield, having been imported from West Germany. After machining, it was re-exported to Mexico.

One of Brazil's largest heavy-haulage companies is Superpesa who have always shown a strong allegiance to American-built tractor units. Here a Kenworth 850 tractor, equipped with a detachable ballast weight, hauls a large transformer on the 300-tonne capacity Cometto girder frame trailer.

slung between them, each end being mounted on a pedestal fixed on the two-axle, hydrostatically-powered module. The girder frame will take loads of up to 500 tonnes, and was built originally by the German trailer specialists, Waggon Union, as a road/rail transporter. The girder frame, complete with load, can be transferred from the road transporters to railway bogies as requirements dictate.

Further north, in Finland, another Scheuerle self-propelled transporter can be found operating with Imatran Voima. This consists of two hydrostatically driven power cars, each of which has Scheuerle bogie modules coupled behind with nine axle lines per vehicle. Again the steering and hydraulic suspension systems are retained. This enormous transporter operates with loads up to 500 tonnes on public roads which, in Finland, poses few problems because of the sparse population. The special girder-frame transporter bridge was built for Imatran by Trabosa in Spain.

Going east into European USSR, one can find a British-built twelve-axle Crane-Fruehauf girder-frame trailer, operating with three 6 × 4 Scammell Contractors and designed for loads of 300 tonnes. This was purchased initially to transport transformers for Russian power stations. Heavy-haulage equipment actually manufactured in the USSR is limited in quantity and the trailers that can be seen

bear a remarkable resemblance to European designs. Heavy tractors imported from the West are used for the really heavy hauls inside the USSR, although the Kraz 255 6 × 6 is often employed on loads approaching 60 tonnes gtw. Scammell and Magirus Deutz 6 × 6 machines, imported some years ago as part of a massive contract for dump-trucks, take over above these weights and some unusual OeAF 6 × 6 tractors may also be found there. Available tractors of Russian design are directly derived from military types, principally the Maz 8 × 8 missile transporter.

Going further east again, and deeper into Russian territory, a number of specially built Faun HZ40 45/45 6 × 6 tractors, mounted on massive flotation tyres and powered by Deutz engines can be found. These were purchased for use on a natural-gas pipeline and carry giant steel pipes, using a bolster on the tractor and a separate dolly.

Eastern bloc countries tend to make use of Russian military designs for transporting heavy equipment, but Czechoslovakia uses its homebred Tatra vehicles. These are fitted with the company's own V-12 air-cooled diesel engine and are available in several configurations, including 6 × 6 and 8 × 8 types. Both of these and some exquisite German Faun 6 × 6 draw-bar tractors, are operated by the heavy-haulage division of the state transport organisation, CSAD. Scheurle build the modular trailer equipment.

Built in the Netherlands by Floor's Handel, the FTF range of three-axle tractors uses British Motor Panels cab structures and Detroit Diesel power units. Netherlands-based Mammoet Transport, operating on a global basis with their associated fleet of heavy-lift ships, used large numbers of FTFs in association with Scheuerle modular trailer equipment and these vehicles are to be found in many remote areas of the world, engaged in specialised heavy-haulage. Production of the FTF range started in the late 1960s and the vehicles have proved increasingly popular with Dutch heavy-haulage specialists. Recently, an 8 × 4 model was introduced to complement the already extensive range of products.

A design which has experienced changing fortunes is that currently offered by MOL in Belgium. MOL have, for many years, built their own range of heavy

tractors for both the home and export markets. Various types of the Deutz air-cooled engine have been used and Sarens deCoster, a major heavy-haulage operator in Belgium, have operated many MOL tractors in recent years. However, the design in question is that of a 6 × 6 or 8 × 8 tractor, which originated with Willème in France. The Willème manufacturing interests were taken over by Perez et Raimond de Paris (PRP) in the late 1960s. PRP continued to produce the tractors and extended the range, offering several vehicles of different capacities. Some were produced bearing the Willème name, whereas later machines bore the letters PRP. Engine options included General Motors, Cummins and Mercedes power units, although PRP were at one time agents for Detroit Diesels only. In 1979, PRP were taken over by the giant Creusot-Loire Group, who initially offered an 8 × 8 design for military operations in a tank-transporter role. The vehicle was unusual in that the tank was transported on the back of the long-wheelbase truck rather than on a trailer.

Ultimately, the designs passed to MOL, who still build the vehicles. The MOL TG250 8 × 8 tractor uses the Cummins KT-450 diesel engine, Clark torque-converter and gearbox, with hub-reduction axles by Kessler. Although compact by comparison with some tractors, at just over 8 m (26¼ ft) in length and 3 m (9 ft 10 in) wide, it is larger than many others cur-

Ex-military hardware has always proved popular with heavy haulers and this unusual Kenworth XM194 8 × 8, used by McLeod Trucking, certainly proves up to the task required of it boasting an 800-hp Continental V8 engine! Tri-axle dropframe semi-trailer has a capacity of 200 tonnes.

rently produced in Europe and is nominally rated for 250 tonnes gross train operation. In 1976, specialist trailer manufacturers, Trabosa, in Spain, built two 8 × 8 tractors based on the PRP designs. They were for Spanish operator, Sainnerts operated with multi-axle Trabosa modules moving heavy sections for the Spanish nuclear power programme.

In 1981, Sainnerts joined forces with the American Rigging International Company, well known for their activities with massive crawler transporters around the world. These two companies, in association with four other European heavy-haulage specialist, instigated the design and manufacture of specialist tractors for their own use. Known as Irtex, these are 8 × 8 machines, which are fitted with General Motors power units and the DAF 2800 cab.

For many years, the French trailer specialist, Jean B. Nicolas, had acted in association first with Willème, and then with PRP, in supplying matched tractor-trailer combinations to heavy-haulage operators. A determined and co-ordinated sales effort by both manufacturers resulted in the awarding of a large order from the Republic of China in 1975. This order included several PRP 6 × 6 TG300 tractor units and twelve separate trailer and transporter systems from the French specialist builder, Nicolas. Capacities ran from 100 to 600 tonnes using modular trailers and included a 600-tonne girder-frame unit. Two 150-tonne Nicolas Automas self-propelled transporters completed the prestigious and valuable export order.

Later on, when PRP sold off their design to Mol of Belgium, Nicolas decided to go it alone and to build their own heavy-haulage tractor. This eventually appeared under the name 'Tractomas' and employed a Berliet (Renault) cab and generally Cummins diesel power. Several models were offered, including 6 × 6 and even 8 × 8 configurations, and capacities extended to 300-tonnes 'nominal' gtw. One such Tractomas, equipped with a powerful Cummins KT450, is operated by British operator, Sunter Bros of Northallerton. Now part of United Heavy Transport, Sunters is famous for many things, including having operated, for many years, the beautiful and rare Rotinoff heavy-haulage tractor.

Another name synonymous with heavy haulage is Scammell, whose current range of specialised tractors is based on two main types, the S24 and S26. The S24, introduced in 1980, replaced the Contractor and the venerable Constructor range. Many different models are currently built, all using Cummins NTE 350 engines and automatic or manual transmission, plus torque-converter. Larger models can be rated for 300-tonnes gross and already a number have found their way into overseas fleets, particularly in New Zealand and the Middle East. In the UK, Econofreight operate a pair of drawbar S24s, while Hill's of Botley in Hampshire have a 150-ton model.

The S26 range is similar in appearance to the Leyland Roadtrain normal-haulage tractor and, in fact, utilises the same basic cab structure. The 6 × 4 model has been finding increasing favour with British operators and examples are now operated by Wynn's and Sunter Bros (now joined to form United Navy Transport), Tony Morgan in South Wales, Leicester Heavy Haulage, West of Scotland and others.

The machine has been favourably compared to the German Titan, but British tractors have never sold well in Europe or outside the Commonwealth and its chances of winning against that marque on its home ground are remote.

Exceptions to the 'European is best' philosophy, however, include the Contractors sold to the USSR, another which went to Finland, and a brace which are still used today by the Swedish operator, Binsell. Not surprisingly, Binsell also supports the domestic industry and Volvo tractors, including an interesting N12 250-tonner, are also found in the fleet.

For many years now, American Kenworth units have dominated the oil-industry truck market in the Middle East. The 953, designed specifically to succeed in conditions where others fail, is probably without equal when it comes to the awesome task of hauling giant drilling rigs across the open desert. These trucks are found in large numbers in areas where the going is really tough and only Mack seems capable of producing a close second.

In recent years, however, this absolute domination has been challenged not only by Mercedes, MAN, Berliet (Renault) and Titan but by Japanese types, such as Fuso and Nissan. The bonneted Fuso 6 × 6 tractor has proved extremely versatile, not just in the Middle East, but also at home and throughout the entire Pacific area.

The truly gigantic, double-ended, multi-wheeled transporter built by Hitachi Engineering for the Nippon Express enterprise, Kaelble 8 × 8 tractors operated with a Scheuerle girder-frame trailer and used by the Turkish Electricity Authority, Gerosa of New York and their unique 400-short-ton (363-tonne) capacity Autocar 6 × 4 tractor, two special Hendrickson 6 × 6 tractors used with a Talbert trailer in Egypt, Kenworth's massive 993 with vast, multi-modular Trabosa transporters in Spain, Chris Miller's Mack and Cometto outfit in the UK, Zwagerman's Titan and Mercedes tractors in the Netherlands – all these are superb examples of highly specialised, individually tailored heavy-haulage vehicles. They may be only a few examples of many thousands in use around the world admittedly, but they are proof that, wherever one looks, one can find a contribution made to our modern, industrialised society by the true giants of the industry.

ALL THE COMFORTS OF HOME

The USA is still a land of all that is bigger and brighter in the world and its best qualities are free enterprise and the possibility of self-realisation. That even holds true for the modern trucker. Though life on the interstate highways is not always as rosy as it is made out to be by some of the outside press, the American independent trucker could indeed be called a modern-day cowboy, crossing the endless plains and snowclad mountain ranges on his 'iron horse'.

Compared with that of other countries, the US machinery is certainly bigger, more powerful and a great deal more eye-catching with its spectacular paintwork and acres of dazzling chrome – and the drivers are often as colourful! These contemporary heroes of

the free road have come a long way since the '40s and '50s, struggling with lots of paperwork, regulations and more restrictions than you could imagine. For many, it has not been easy to make a decent living out of long-haul trucking, despite their fabulous equipment and 'last of the cowboys' image.

Until a few years ago it was virtually impossible for a big rig to haul cross-country without encountering,

One of the most dazzling reefers on American roads is this spectacular 1984 Peterbilt 359 longnose with 46-ft Polar-American trailer. Owned by independent trucker George Rogers, the rig draws attention wherever it goes.

A microwave oven, refrigerator with ice-tray, hot and cold running water and a chemical toilet are just a few of the amenities which are built into the topline sleepers of today.

somewhere along the line, an over-eager state trooper or weight station inspector, who would book the unwary trucker on the spot for being either overlength or overweight. Many independents, as the US owner-drivers are called, have thus forked out big bucks for state fines, especially in the conservative eastern legislatures. It is generally known that a large number of truckers choose to spend several hours more behind the wheel, and drive a few hundred miles around, rather than stand the chance of being thrown into jail in some of the notorious states with anti-truck problems.

With the powerful truck-regulating body, the Interstate Commerce Commission, adopting a more flexible approach a few years ago, and the introduction of the Surface Transportation Act in 1982, a lot has been done to improve long interstate road haulage. Though the new measures were not all welcomed because they also comprised much higher taxes on trucks, components, tyres, fuel and registration fees, at least the burden of forty-eight sets of differing state laws regarding weights and dimensions of commercial vehicles was relieved. From then on, only the length of the trailer or doubles was limited. This means that, today, a semi-trailer with a generous maximum length of 48 ft (14.6 m) can be pulled behind any tractor, irrespective of its length. In other words, there is no longer a maximum overall length limit for the complete combination on major interstate and other highways throughout the USA. In many states, however, it is still not possible to operate these long units on every type of road system and some local legislators are even fighting the new federal decisions in court.

For the American independent truck driver, it has so far proved a big boon and most Class 8 truck manufacturers will tell you that the market for long-nosed conventionals has increased dramatically since mid-1982. Apart from the advantages in purchase price compared to a high-spec cabover, a conventional truck has better riding characteristics, is much more service-friendly and is a safer bet when caught in a head on collision. Besides, and this might be the most important thing for many self-respecting owner-drivers of the Yankee-roads, a big mean looking conventional is way more 'macho' than a plain cabover.

Thanks to the revision of federal highway laws, the American trucker no longer needs to put up with stressful schedules and strained marriages. Now he can escape the middle-of-the-road conformity by outfitting his money-machine as a mobile travel home and ask the lady to join him in style. The permitting of any length of tractor, while still maintaining maximum precious cargo space, allows independent truckers to specify the most elaborate Kenworth or Peterbilt with separate sleeper boxes that are bigger and more luxurious than ever. These huge self-contained homes-away-from-home offer the more successful husband-and-wife teams all the con-

T his Kenworth Aerodyne is powered by a 450-hp Detroit Diesel coupled to an Allison Automatic plus four-speed Spicer gearbox. Equipped with Double Eagle's 120-in (3-m) long sleeper the incredible outfit costs $170,000.

venience, privacy and comforts for which they could possibly wish.

At a recent famous International Truck Show in Anaheim, California, more manufacturers than ever presented a few dozen types of sleeper, from the standard 36 in (90 cm) sleeper box to the most incredible 140 in (355 cm) living quarters. Able, All American, Alumi Bunk, Bentz, Booth, Paramount, Voyager, Liv Lab and Double Eagle are just a few major names that pop up everywhere, with the Indiana-based Double Eagle Industries undoubtedly the most famous and prestigious manufacturer of custom-built truck sleepers in the world. The quality and level of workmanship is unsurpassed and the company has built up a great reputation among America's top in the owner-operator league. When you ask Mike Stroud (aged 53) of South El Monte, California, why he has specced out his immaculate black long-nosed Peterbilt with the biggest sleeper ever built on a conventional by Double Eagle Industries, he answers: 'They are simply making the best sleepers in the world there, and for a price they will get you anything you ask for!'

His 475-hp 'Pete' rides on a 302-in (767-cm) wheel base, which was the length needed to accommodate the 120 × 80 × 94 in (305 × 203 × 239 cm) sleeper cab of the Aerodyne type. The completely aluminium sleeper is kitted out with every imaginable convenience and looks more like a topclass motor home

inside than a truck. Entering the 'recreational area' from the cab, you first encounter a neat and cosy corner where a swivelling lounge chair lets you watch the colour TV or the built-in video system. Or just relax after a hard day's driving with a good book from one of the many cabinets and listen to the super quality of the stereo hi-fi system before moving on to the kitchen department, where an electric coffee-maker is waiting. Or grab some food from the refrigerator, and place it in the microwave oven for a few minutes. When time comes to 'hit the sack', Mike Stroud looks for the Porta-Potti chemical toilet, washes himself with either cold or hot running water from the kitchen tap and then stretches down on his 50 × 80 in (127 × 203 cm) large Airride double bed. Indeed, even a kingsized bed, that floats on air and fades out even the worst of bumps, if the truck should ride on through the night with a second driver, is also one of the amazing options available from Double Eagle Industries. Stroud usually hits the road alone but, on some of his 7,000-mile (11,265-km) hauls from California to eastern Canada, his wife accompanies him and quite often he takes along his fishing gear and throws out a line in one of the great Canadian rivers when they have to wait for a backload. 'Sometimes I unhitch the semi and drive my tractor onto a campground and simply hook up to their convenience system. You should see the faces of the recreational vehicle (RV) fraternity down there when I sit the weekend out in my luxurious "truck home"!'

'King Pin' and 'Queen Bee', as husband-and-wife team Ralph and Betty Campbell from Idaho are known over the CB, have driven heavy trucks together for over 30 years and can now call themselves the proud owners of a big Freightliner with 400-hp Cummins diesel and equipped with a giant Voyager sleeper. Making everyday work more like a vacation, this hard-charging couple chose the ultimate in trucksleepers currently available from this well-known Recreational Vehicle manufacturer from Washington State.

The one-piece moulded fibreglass unit even has such amenities as a galley and dinette, so that you can eat in you own inhouse restaurant or take a shower at your convenience in your own facilities. Included is a

6-gallon (23-l) hot-water tank with a quick-recovery heating system and, to make the picture complete, an optional recirculating toilet that requires no additional water is available to please even the most exacting driving team of today.

The Florida-based Liv Lab Inc. is another producer of super-sleepers and has a top model on offer that challenges the most luxurious RV motor homes on the road in features and comforts but, of course, at a price. Quality does not come cheap and a big very elaborately outfitted 'truck travel home' can cost anything up to a massive $40,000. For that kind of money you are really on top though.

Standard features often include hot and cold running water, a microwave oven and two-burner hob, refrigerator, kitchen sink, chemical toilet, interior table, several cabinets and lockers, full-size wardrobe

Owner Mike Stroud specified the largest sleeper from Double Eagle for his conventional. This black beauty is the ultimate truck-travel-home for its owner and saves him many motel bills.

with mirrors, queen-sized double bed, air conditioning and heating system, etc. Some units even have provisions for sewage and waste-water storage, laundry chute and automatic vacuum cleaning throughout the living quarters. Carpeting, insulation and ventilation can also match the best in RV-camper outfits and, naturally, the entertainment area is certainly just as impressive with a colour TV, stereo hi-fi set, video system, 40-channel CB and much more to make life on the road enjoyable.

Californians Dan and Robin Campbell represent the younger truck generation, but have done extremely

Making work more like a vacation in this Voyager 'travel home' complete with dinette, galley, shower and flush toilet.

well so far and their 'No Excuses'-christened Aerodyne Kenworth cabover, with 120-in (305-cm) Double Eagle super-sleeper, must be seen to be believed. This friendly and well-educated couple transport high-tech equipment for Bekins Van Lines across the American continent and, being on the road more than 90% of their lives, they do not even own a home. That is, not a static brick-type one, because their mobile working-cum-living quarters on the back of the big Kenworth must be the best money can buy in this respect. While on the road, Robin can serve almost any dinner in the complete kitchenette and, after the driving chores, the couple can relax back in the plush interior to watch pre-recorded movies. In the meantime, the fully automatic air conditioning and heating system ensure a pleasant temperature at all times, including the engine block to prevent it from freezing in wintertime!

Taking about 2 weeks for a return trip from coast to coast, with several pick-up and delivery points in between, the Campbells save a fortune on motel and restaurant bills with the truck sleeper. 'If we like it is

possible to run from one side of the country to the other in a mere three days taking turns behind the wheel', says Dan Campbell. 'We do not lose time looking for accommodation or foodstops and even our business is done right from out of the cab with the help of a longreach cellular telephone'.

Rigs fitted out with so much hardware cannot rely on the truck's own power, especially not while parked up, so most units have an auxiliary engine built neatly underneath the sleeper compartment. There are 110 V generators keeping a constant watch on the batteries, and the equipment also comes in handy when working on the truck with outside electrical tools. If that is not enough, many of the more elaborately fitted out 'truck homes' can be connected into mainlines anywhere. The modern sleepers are benefiting marriages as well as budgets and, if you ask truck drivers on the road what they usually dislike most about their gear-jamming life, then often the answer is loneliness and truckstop junkfood. So taking the wife along as a driving partner and installing an upscale new super-sleeper, can make life in an eighteen-wheeler a lot more enjoyable.

Even today, a larger number of transport companies will recognise the need to improve the welfare of their drivers and prefer to hire husband-and-wife teams. 'Couples drive better and safer with much more concern for the equipment', says Pete Carroll of Circle C Trucking in Michigan. 'For our 80 reefer trucks we have mostly husband and wife teams, and they are regarded as the best and most courteous drivers around'. This famous company probably has the best-looking fleet in the nation and, as one California state trooper recently remarked, when one of the husband-and-wife teams, with a magnificent Peterbilt, pulled in for a check: 'Circle C's rigs beautify America!' And there cannot be better advertising for this young company from the east; after all the most mind-blowing equipment is said to originate on the West Coast.

American trucks are more than ever a blending of art and machine, occupying a very special place in the world of road transport. With a sound insight of the modern truck business, and the right approach to working long and hard, the individual can still make it big in the land of plenty, living as luxuriously on the road as others do at home. Despite very steep purchase prices and sky-high operating costs, the lure of the open road is still there and many of today's free-spirited independents cannot resist it. Thanks to the new truck laws and the insight of the sleeper-cab industries, at least they can now save the marriage and take the whole family along if need be.

According to George and Pat Rogers of Tucson, Arizona, who share the cross-country driving in one of the most eye-catching reefer trucks you have ever seen, the only drawback of operating such sophisticated and expensive equipment is the tremendous amount of attention you get on Uncle Sam's roads. 'Some fourwheelers keep on hanging there in the other lane just to have a better look at our rig and that can be pretty dangerous at times, they just forget about all the other traffic around!'

The image of the American King-of-the-Road is still very much alive, but he now rides with his Princess and spends his time in a palace-on-wheels. . . .

LIQUIDS, POWDERS AND GASES

Blood and beer, shampoo and sewage, hot, steaming chocolate and super-cooled liquid nitrogen; all these commodities are transported over our highways in tankers. Not at the same time and in the same tank of course, but in tanks which, although similar in appearance, are built to carry different loads and have very special and individual characteristics.

The whole business of tank-truck transportation is highly specialised and the vehicles used in it are fascinating as a result. By their very nature, tankers are attractive, whether mounted on a rigid truck or on semi-trailers, and this feature is often accentuated by the polished stainless steel used in their construction. Access ladders, catwalks and manhole covers add interest to the tank itself and items such as air suspension and anti-skid systems are more likely to be found on tankers than on any other vehicle, in deference to the value of the load carried or perhaps to the potential danger of a noxious substance escaping in the event of an accident.

Because of their specialised nature, tankers are usually owned and operated by own-account or private carriers to haul their own product. Typical examples are the fuel tankers operated by Esso; these vehicles are built solely to haul one type of liquid load from bulk fuel storage areas to service stations. Loading is done mainly through manlids at the top of the tank (although Esso recently took delivery of some new, experimental bottom-load tanker trailers) and discharge *via* outlet ports at the bottom, gravity being the medium employed. Other similar examples are the beer tankers owned by Guinness and detergent tankers operated by the Unilever group.

Early tanks were of rivetted construction until welding developed sufficiently to enable them to withstand the rigours of rough road use. Mild steel used to be the main material used in tank construction but this was of limited use in its manufactured form. Some form of coating or lining had to be used in situations where the contents of the tank might attack the tank interior surface, e.g. with most acids, while in other cases the steel itself could affect the load, e.g. rust and pitting of the tank surface might harm foodstuffs being carried.

The development of aluminium as a tank-construction material opened up new areas of possibilities in the matter of commodities carried, for aluminium is not subject to the same corrosion as mild steel and, for the carriage of some materials, requires no special coating. It is easier to keep clean, suitable for many foodstuffs and much lighter than steel. Drawbacks have been due to the difficulties of welding aluminium and the need to provide greater support or stiffening because of its comparative weakness for a given section.

As the welding of stainless steel was perfected, so this material too began to fulfill a need in tank fabrication for the conveyance of certain foodstuffs. Its ability to withstand certain cleaning agents and its great inherent strength and hardness all combined to provide an important advance in road-tank construction.

The shape of tanks has undergone a major change in recent years, with the established cylindrical barrel with dished ends being challenged by a variety of new designs, each with relevant advantages. While the common cylindrical tank is still widely used, it does have certain limitations with regard to size, and hence capacity. The size of a cylinder is bounded by its diameter and its length and these are linked with the

Claimed to be the largest bulk tanker in Europe, and probably one of the largest in use anywhere, is this massive Briab-built truck-trailer combination operated by Ebenol in Sweden.

overall legal dimensions of trucks and cannot be exceeded; thus the capacity is limited. Where there is a need to increase the capacity of a tank because the volume is full long before the legal gross weight is reached, then there is a need to vary the sectional shape of the body in order to contain the additional load. This is achieved by going away from the accepted plain cylinder section tank and making it a vertically stretched oval, or dropping the belly of the tank towards the ground in the area between the front and rear wheels if possible.

So we find, for certain loads, shapes such as elliptical, D-shaped, squared-off ellipse and, the most recent to emerge, rectangular. All these shapes have seen use for certain liquids and powders, but they cannot be used for loads which are either loaded, emptied or transported under pressure, for the cylinder maintains its shape under pressure while other shapes may not. For certain gases which are carried under extreme pressure, it may be necessary to use a spherical tank or several small-diameter cylinders made of seamless high-grade steel.

One of the undoubted advantages of tanker operation as far as the driver is concerned is that the load generally flows on and off the vehicle without him having to do anything more energetic than turning a few release valves or opening hatches. Certainly most liquids are far easier to load than other commodities and it is little wonder that drivers employed on regular tank work guard their jobs jealously.

Some loads are rather less pleasant than others, however, more obvious examples being corrosive acids and waste liquids known as 'effluents'. These liquids have their own special qualities which, in addition to requiring specially built tanks, also demand that great care be taken during loading and unloading procedures. Corrosive acids are carried in tanks with special linings capable of withstanding the effects of the liquid, while outlet cocks and fittings are usually in special alloys which do not suffer from attack by the load.

Loading effluents is obviously a most unpleasant task and the secret here is to somehow encourage the liquid to load itself without the need for it to be handled in any way. A vacuum tank is generally employed here; a donkey engine mounted on the tank drives an air compressor which can be used to create a vacuum. As the pressure inside the tank is reduced, the effluent flows into it. Discharging the load is carried out by reversing the procedure.

Tankers are an expensive part of road-transport fleets because the construction demands high-quality materials put together with an equally high level of technical expertise. Today the majority of tanks are of chassis-less construction, the tank itself being made of sufficient strength along its length to withstand the bending and twisting that occurs in service. Articulated tanks are suitably strengthened around the attachment points for fifth wheel, landing legs and suspension points. A tank mounted on a rigid chassis can be supported much more easily, although some form of flexible attachment may be necessary in order to absorb any twisting in the truck chassis frame before it can distort the tank and perhaps cause cracking of the shell.

Where tanks are made to carry loads at either higher or lower temperatures than that of the surrounding air, they are suitably insulated; or, in

C lassic style of the bonneted FBW is clearly illustrated in this brilliant example of a truck and trailer operated by Indermuhle of Zurzach in Switzerland. Hazardous chemicals are transported in the tanks, but, because of the engine's power output, gross weight is restricted to 26 tonnes.

extreme cases, have heating coils placed inside the tank barrel. Naturally, tar and chocolate need to be kept in a molten state whilst being transported so that they will flow easily for unloading. Drivers in charge of tankers carrying such loads must be conversant with the factors affecting the carriage of them as delays may cause partial solidifying of the load. Where temperatures or pressures are vital, tankers are fitted with gauges and these should be visible from the driving position, some even being printed in reverse so that they are easily read through the rear-view mirror!

Driving a tanker is not considered to require any special skill but there is one load which does indeed take some getting used to from the driver's point of view. Oddly, the liquid in question is nothing more sinister than milk, but the facts are that, although the liquid itself is neither harmful nor unpleasant, the tanks used to transport it are different from most others in that they do not have compartments or baffles. As a result of this construction, the liquid load surges back and forth in the tank regardless of how smoothly gear changes are made or how delicately braking and acceleration are performed. The experienced driver is accustomed to timing gearshifts and braking carefully to allow for the effects of the load, but to the novice, the force of a few thousand gallons of milk pushing him around when he least expects it is a new and not altogether pleasant sensation.

The size, shape, construction and general appearance of tanks varies enormously, adding to their interest. Capacities range from a few hundred gallons,

B-train double-tank combinations are popular in eastern Canada where operators appreciate the safety and payload of these huge machines. Built by Hutchinon Industries, this combination employs singles on the trailers, a lifting rearmost axle and offers a gross weight of almost 62 tonnes.

on small trucks used to deliver heating fuel to private homes, up to aircraft refuellers at the other end of the spectrum which can haul 20,000 Imperial gallons (which is equivalent to about 91,000 litres). For normal road tankers operated at the legal maximum of around 38 to 40 tonnes (as in Europe and North America for example) an average capacity could be said to be in the region of 6,000 Imperial gallons (27,300 litres), at least for liquid loads.

Where the products carried are not so heavy as liquids, and this is particularly so with regard to certain powders and pellets used in the plastics industry, then it becomes necessary for tank designers to increase the capacity of the vehicle to suit. The basic idea of a box with radiused corners with easy-clean characteristics, plus a shape which lends itself to easy discharge, are useful parameters.

Sometimes the shape of the tank has been designed to assist with loading or discharging of the contents, a case in point being the double-cone layout of certain cement tanks. This design helps the unloading by bringing the outlet point to the lowest part of the body so that the contents naturally fall towards it. Unfortunately, cement, flour and other bulk fine powders have a tendency to shake down and solidify during a journey, so a system of agitation or aeration has to be incorporated which, by movement and air pressure, helps loosen up and fluidise the load and help it along the discharge pipe.

For maximum cubic capacity within the broad shape of a cylinder, some tanks are narrowed over the coupling area or rear bogie and this gives rise to the 'babies bottle' title for their shape. Other designs consist of a row of squat vertical tanks, or even spheres, while yet another connects these tanks to form a large rounded tank at the top but with several separate bottom outlets. Various shapes are used for a variety of loads which, because of their own particular properties, are best handled in a completely closed tank rather than the regular open-tipper or dump-style of bodywork.

Different techniques are used to load and discharge bulk tanks, including gravity, vacuum, air pressure, pumping, CO_2 pressure, tipping and blowing. Loading may be from the same level or from above or below ground and the same circumstances can apply to unloading. Some tanks are equipped with tipping gear and here the method of unloading is simply to tip the entire tank in the same way that a dump-body is lifted. Dry cement powder, sand, flour and animal feed are just some of the many commodities handled in this way.

Early in the 1970s, prototype tanks were produced in glass-reinforced plastic (GRP) for the transport of various commodities. Advantages were said to be light weight and facility of quick cleaning, thus enabling differing cargoes to be carried in swift succession.

It was not until 1978 that the first GRP tanker gained acceptance for carrying flammable liquids, such as motor fuel, and then it was of double-skinned construction with an ample insulating filler of polyurethane foam. This revolutionary design reverted to the early design feature of rectangular tank sections, although this time in GRP, not like the old rivetted steel tanks. By producing the tanks in sec-

tional units, each one separate and insulated from its neighbour and with the base down low where possible, it was possible to provide a very compact vehicle with a low centre of gravity. The smooth, clean outside surface presented by the finish skin of plastics promotes a good image, is easy to clean and helps reduce air drag. Although the whole tanker is largely made of plastics, the manlids, faucets, fifth-wheel rubbing-plate and running-gear supports are all in metal and carefully moulded in during manufacture. Exhaustive tests were carried out on the tanker before a petroleum licence was granted for the design to carry flammable liquids.

Less stringent regulations apply to tankers carrying non-flammable liquids and the GRP tanks are well suited to most cargoes, except those having the ability to attack the surface of the plastics. Naturally, gravity loading and discharging are used with this type of material and the tank should not be subjected to excessive pressures.

It was not so long ago that certain acids were transported in glass carboys, which were easy to keep clean and useful for small deliveries. These clear glass bottles were shrouded in natural straw and contained in an outer covering of steel mesh. Plastic containers have taken the place of the old glass carboys for the handling of small amounts, but metal tankers with the necessary protection are used for the bulk movements of dangerous liquids.

Although the tanks themselves are quite adequate for the everyday transport and handling of the products for which they were designed, a smooth cylinder of stainless steel, or other special material used in tank construction, cannot be expected to contain the load should the truck be involved in a high-speed impact or rollover incident.

Unusual example of a dual-purpose tanker is this Canadian rig operated by Chapman Transport, part of the Canadian National group. An obvious disadvantage is the very high platform height and subsequent high centre of gravity for deck loads.

Guard rails are fitted to tanks to protect the protruding, and often delicate, items, such as cocks, faucets, valves, manlids, outlets, gauges and pumps. Larger areas, such as the vulnerable rear end, can be protected with a stout rear bumper or under-run guard, while side damage is warded off by sections of Armco similar to motorway crash barriers. Substantial rollbars are welded to the tank at front and rear to help protect the vital top-mounted items, such as filling cocks and manlids.

But all this protection is good only up to a point and the real protection of the tank and its contents rest in the capable hands of the drivers, backed up by the loaders and maintenance men. All those involved in the handling of hazardous loads and toxic substances receive regular training and instruction regarding the safe handling of the products. Instructions on procedures to be adopted at loading points, customers' premises and other discharge points are regularly dispensed, as are details of loads, their recognition, policy of handling leakages, reporting accidents and advising the emergency services.

The wide adoption of the Hazchem scheme for the speedy identification, labelling and safe handling of dangerous substances has helped everyone concerned, but most particularly the emergency services who have to cope with the safety of the public at large when any spillages occur. The acceptance of an easily identifiable scheme, coupled with higher levels of training for all those involved with toxic substances,

has helped regain public confidence, which was at a low ebb after a couple of major accidents. Whilst there are some who feel that dangerous loads should not travel by road, it is difficult to imagine the present level of civilisation without the many chemical substances which can be hazardous to Man, and which we use every day.

One of the most interesting bulk-tank vehicles currently in service is that operated by a Swedish company called Ebe Energy Systems. This manufacturer converts waste wood products, such as sawdust and chippings, into a fuel known as Ebenol. The fuel is burned in specially modified furnaces to produce heat for factories and is claimed to be far cheaper than more conventional oil-based products.

Ebenol is a lightweight powder and, as such, its movement in large quantities posed problems for the manufacturer. The solution was finally provided by the bulk-tank manufacturer, Briab, whose engineers designed a truck-trailer rig capable of hauling $128\,m^3$ $(4,520\,ft^3)$ of product in eleven conical compartments. The vehicle, capable of grossing up to 61 tonnes but restricted by Swedish law to 51.4 tonnes, is built to the absolute maximum dimensions of 2.6 m in width,

24 m in overall length and 4.5 m in height ($8\frac{1}{2}$ ft × $78\frac{3}{4}$ ft × $14\frac{3}{4}$ ft). It is considered by Briab to be the largest bulker of its type in use anywhere in the world and there can be no doubt that this hugely impressive vehicle is an awesome spectacle, even when seen among Sweden's already larger-than-average trucks. Unloading the steel tanks is done using a Wade compressor to pressurise each compartment and this process is speeded up by using a process patented by Briab which they term 'fluidising'.

Tanks may well be interesting and spectacular but, for the operator, they represent certain very obvious operational disadvantages. For a start, whether installed on a rigid truck or built on a semi-trailer, a tank is an extremely expensive item. As already discussed, despite the most rigorous cleaning methods, no one tank will accept several different kinds of liquid or powdered load, so there are limits as to where it may be employed. By the very nature of the business, tanks are loaded in one direction only. To the operator, this is one stumbling block which it is almost impossible to overcome. There have been attempts to offset this disadvantage, with some operators prepared to accept a 'compromise' vehicle capable of performing more than one function.

These vehicles, known as 'platypus' tanks, are utilised only where long hauls are commonplace or where an operator takes a regular liquid load in one direction and collects a fairly dense, solid commodity for the return. The platypus is a genuine dual-purpose

Although absent from the truck-building scene for over a decade, this Hayes tractor (featuring a Mack F700 cab) nevertheless represents the energy and efficiency that is so much a part of the North American trucking industry.

truck, featuring a low-profile tank, with regular loading and discharge facilities, which doubles as a platform or flat deck capable of taking palletised goods: timber for example, for the return journey.

These vehicles have drawbacks since they are clearly not designed to offer the absolute maximum capacity for either product. And they are not legal in some countries, their construction contravening either road-traffic law or, in some cases, legislation introduced by apparently unrelated government departments, such as the Ministry of Agriculture, Fisheries and Food in the UK.

Where such combinations are legal, however, they can be used to considerable advantage. One such situation exists in western British Columbia, where Wells Cartage, a small trucking company specialising in the movement of wood products, operates a custom-built B-train designed to haul liquid resin in the tanks in one direction and plywood in bundles on the trailer decks on the return haul.

Powered by a Western Star cabover tractor, the 63-tonne B-train is a remarkable vehicle. The low-profile tanks feature deep drop-well sections between axle groupings and, because of the very high specific gravity of the resin, are able to accept a full load, despite their relatively small volume. As a result of the low overall height of the tanks (the platform is only 51 cm (20 in) higher than a normal platform deck), a very large load of plywood can be hauled on the return load. Axle loadings are met as a result of the carefully-

When the maximum weight for five-axle artics in the UK was increased to 38 tonnes, some interesting 'specials' found their way into service. Examples included this White Road Commander with second-steer axle located ahead of the driving axle.

This Swiss Saurer carries a six-compartment FFA tank for the transport of wine in bulk. With a capacity of 18,000 litres, the elliptical section tank is unloaded by gravity.

For handling gases under extreme pressure, it is necessary to construct the tank from heavy-section cylinders with inverted dished ends for strength. This Seddon-Atkinson outfit is operated by Shell.

specified Knight trailers and, as with all B-train rigs operated in British Columbia, a self-steered, air-lift axle is located towards the rear of the leading semi-trailer. A twin-turbo Cummins NTC 475-hp Big Cam 3 diesel, driving through a fifteen-speed Fuller deep-reduction RT15615 transmission to a 20-tonne Rockwell SSHD bogie makes up the mechanical specification.

Western Star cabover tractors are in themselves extremely interesting vehicles, being built by the Volvo-White Corporation, but marketed and sold through Canadian and American Western Star distributors.

The history of the company is complicated; Western Star at one time formed part of Canada's White Truck group, but became an independently owned company once Volvo bought out the White Motor Corporation. Today, Western Star produce a wide range of heavy-duty Class-8 vehicles in Canada, including a tough and respected line of three-axle conventional tractor units. But, rather oddly, their

In the UK, Imperial Chemical Industries use ISO space-frame tankers for the handling of certain products. Here a heavily-constructed tank for the transport of gas under extreme pressure leaves the Mond Division works bound for a railhead.

cabover production is left entirely to Volvo-White. This co-operation is best illustrated in the product literature for the two companies, where identical brochures extol the virtues of the Volvo-White High Cabover and the Western Star High Cabover. Really close inspection of the illustrations in the brochures reveals two tiny differences, the first that the White logo is missing on the Western Star brochure while the Western Star boasts quarter fenders carrying its logo. The vehicle is obviously the same one, so it seems likely that a touch-up artist was employed to create subtle differences on the two catalogues. Even more odd is the fact that the recently introduced Volvo 'slash' across the grille is retained on all West-

ern Star cabovers and that the manufacturer's plate refers to the truck as a pure, unadulterated Volvo-White product!

Contrasting starkly with the expensive and sophisticated equipment used to move loads of sherry from the vineyards of Spain, or whisky from the pure-water areas of Scotland, are the tiny tanks used in Third-World countries to transport that most valuable of all liquids: drinking water. Many regions are still without their own local supplies and rely totally on water being trucked in from the nearest sources. Most vehicles employed in this vital work are small two-axle rigids, capable of hauling 1,500 gallons, and many are still unloaded using only gravity feed or small hand pumps. Despite their simplicity and modest capacity, their value to those people desperate for water cannot be overstated. They may be nothing more than a large water barrel on wheels, but that, of course, was how the whole idea of today's interesting and diversified road-tanker business got started.

CLOSE THAT GAP!

One sphere of truck operation that has undergone changes in basic design concepts is that of drawbar outfits. The early steam vehicles always had an even older, converted horsedrawn trailer hitched up behind and this primitive idea has been perpetuated until very recently.

With the introduction of the diesel engine in the 1930s, trucks became powerful enough to pull one or two trailers, thereby increasing the load capacity and making road transport the most economical form of transportation.

In many countries, it was possible to assemble commercial vehicles made up of as many units as one would think feasible on a specific route, taking into account any problems regarding terrain and the weather that might be encountered. Notorious among these giant combinations are the snaking outfits, made up of seven or eight trailers, which crossed the Australian deserts in the late 1940s, while the Germans led in Europe with their massive, long-bonneted *Lastkraftwagen*, handling two or three chunky drawbar trailers on the then new '*autobahnen*'.

With the rise in number of vehicles in most civilised countries during the 1960s, the really big and, in particular overlength, multi-trailer combinations gradually disappeared as various governments set new standards for commercial-goods transport operations. European haulage companies were hard hit and profits fell considerably under the new stringent maximum weight and length laws. It was a hard time, with overall length restricted to approximately 18 m (59 ft) for truck-trailer combinations in most European countries and this meant a usable load space of no more than 14 m (46 ft). In recent years, the result has been that, with low-density cargo, the load cubes out before the permitted 38-tonnes gross weight is reached, this gcw figure being widely accepted in Europe.

Now that the pressures of intense competition, coupled with high fuel costs, have forced in-depth study of overall vehicle design, fresh new ideas have blossomed and good standards of high capacity within the confines of current legal overall dimensions, plus a bonus of less drag, have emerged.

By clever manipulation of the towing gear, it is possible to reduce the wasted space between truck and trailer by almost half that previously necessary. With the historic designs of towing gear, the towing hook at the extreme rear end of the vehicle dragged the apex of an A-frame-shaped drawbar, which was hinged to the trailer turntable, which carried the front wheels of the trailer. This layout demanded a space between truck and trailer sufficient to allow the outfit to be jack-knifed without the two units colliding.

Recent designs include offerings by Ackermann-Fruehauf, Kassbohrer, Peitz, Contar, Orthaus, Graf, Doll, Wackenhut and Kogel, and the main concept of these designs is to provide a mechanical means of keeping truck and trailer close-coupled whilst in the straight-ahead position, but with a wider gap provision which comes into play as the outfit is manoeuvred.

Whilst the various trailer and body manufacturers were busy working out the technical problems of the variable drawbars and coupling designs, some well-known truck builders had started feasibility studies with the idea of creating more load space by mounting sleeper sections on top of the cab instead of behind the driver's seat. Back in the 1930s, several US long-distance trucks had been fitted with experimental top-sleeper and close-coupled full trailer was the integrated outfit introduced several years ago by a combin-

The first continental European design of both top-sleeper and close-coupled full trailer was the integrated outfit introduced several years ago by a combination of West German companies, and intended for the high-volume market, such as furniture manufac-

This DAF-Ginaf MAG2800 with underfloor engine and three steering axles is one of the recent radical designs which allow the transport of five air-cargo containers in one truckload.

turers and household removals. This fresh-looking, high-cube, streamlined outfit was developed by Ackermann, Fruehauf and Daimler-Benz. This 'alternative system for economical transport' as it was labelled or *Grossraum Lastzug* (GLZ) had a healthy cubic capacity of $100\,m^3$ (about $130\,yd^3$) with a cargo length of $15.4\,m$ ($50\frac{1}{2}\,ft$), which was around 10% more than the usual truck-and-trailer outfit. Another innovative feature of the GLZ unit was the possibility to load right through from the rear of the trailer to the front of the truck. The front of the trailer simply opened up and, with the narrow gap in between the units, the straight truck could be quickly loaded without the need to uncouple.

Though the overall gross weight of these first high-volume combinations to appear on continental roads was rather low, at around 27 tonnes gcw, very soon models with higher axle capacities evolved from a variety of manufacturers. The concept appealed to other branches of the trucking industry too and, in particular, the expedited shipment specialists were interested. For example, the shipment of air cargo between the major European cities is made by truck not plane, from the overseas arrival point to the final destination. There are various reasons for this, though the lower tonne-kilometre cost of truck transport is a major factor.

Specifically for this type of shipment, DAF and MAN have teamed up with various body builders to manufacture high-volume truck-and-trailer combinations with such unusual features as underfloor-mounted turbo-charged diesel engines and setback or steering tag-axles, plus of course the ubiquitous top-sleeper. Using such space-saving methods, these special designs are able to carry standard, widebody, air containers and to cram in five, whereas conventional trucks can manage only four. Recently, one Dutch body builder began offering a combination that will hold up to seven air-cargo containers. The secret of the ability to do this lies in the drawbar trailer, which has a spread of three axles all fitted with low-profile tyres, but of very high carrying capacity. The air-cargo containers are stacked two high in this new and revolutionary unit and, with it riding on six axles, total legal weights in its domestic Netherlands can be as high as 50 tonnes gcw.

DAF's unique MAG2800 model, developed in collaboration with specialist builder Ginaf, is still the basis for many air-cargo container vehicles and, fitted with a 132-cm (52-in) cab and roof-mounted top-sleeper, it is the mainstay of the KLM Airlines road-

By the use of hydraulic trombone-type trailer couplings, Scania and Kalmar-Lagab have managed to utilise the large capacity of 24-m (79 ft) rigs to the extreme for TNT-Ipec in Sweden.

going fleet. The very short cab used on this outfit does not allow the normal positioning of the engine below the cab, so DAF's engineers installed one of their horizontal bus engines 'amidships' between the axles. To make regular maintenance of the power unit easier, it can be hydraulically lowered. The three-axle truck has only the rear axle driven, with both front axle and second axle being steered. The rigid truck is coupled to a drawbar trailer which has a fixed and a steering axle, and the geometry of the hook-up allows a gap between truck and trailer of only 55 cm (21½ in). With its five axles in total, the combination has a legal gross weight of 42 tonnes. This ingenious

vehicle design is only one example of the DAF range developed in close co-operation with the body-building industry for the transport of light, voluminous goods. There are also special models today for the transport of heavier cargo which occupies a lot less floor space and, in some cases, gross weights can go right up to 50 tonnes gcw.

Various combinations of engine, gearbox and rear-axle ratios, matched to provide the required performance, are available from DAF and, though some chassis are of less radical design than the MAG2800 mentioned above, all the offerings can be fitted with the luxurious DAF top-sleeper which will save at least 43 cm in load length over a normal behind-the-cab sleeper layout.

Not many manufacturers have been successful in producing premium and economical high-volume combinations, but the German MAN concern has been busy and can claim to be a market leader in this

A fine example of USA West-Coast hauling is this high-cube capacity close-coupled drawbar outfit. When straight-line driving as here, the two units are drawn close together.

Typical top capacity combination in the Netherlands based on the well-proven MAN 22.321 UNL chassis with underfloor engine-layout. The outfit operates on international haulage so a cabtop sleeper is fitted.

field, too, mainly due to its old ties with the defunct Bussing company who were so renowned for their reliable 'underfloor'-engine-layout chassis, similar to the British Sentinel range. Hence many of the high-cube combination builders will offer designs similar to the DAF-based units, using the proven MAN 22.321/361 UNL chassis as a base. Usually these trucks have a three-axle layout with the third axle tagged and steering; naturally the sleeper is mounted on top of the cab in glass fibre in order to save weight and maximise on cargo space. The MAN underfloor-engine models are very popular with drivers, especially when fitted with air-suspended axles all round. The weight distribution is ideal on the rigid truck, even when running empty and, because of the engine positioning way back down the chassis, noise levels are exceptionally low in the cab, even at full throttle.

Not surprisingly, this specialised form of road transport has come on most strongly in the West European countries such as the Netherlands, Belgium, France and West Germany, where road transport is of the utmost importance and competition among operators very fierce. Every cost-conscious haulier endeavours to achieve higher productivity per transport unit and several large truck manufacturers are attempting to penetrate this lucrative new market with adapted, or totally new, designs.

Volvo have introduced a unique bus-derived high-capacity model, the B1OM Cargo with 265 hp under-floor bus diesel engine and a Dutch Berkhof stream-lined cab. This handsome three-axle model, coupled to a tandem-bogie close-coupled trailer, can accommodate five of the air-cargo containers. With full air suspension for the combination, and the engine perched way back beneath the chassis, ride characteristics are very favourable indeed, and, with a mini-mal cab length of just 130 cm (52 in), not much space remains for the driver's needs. In an effort to cram in the maximum amount of freight on the loading deck, some manufacturers seem to forget that the driver still must be able to do his job in complete safety and comfort. Critics say that this particular design has 'standing room' only in the cab. However, most other designs have chosen to adapt one of the truck-builder's standard chassis, albeit with air suspension and additional steering or tag-axles fitted for high-volume operations, and virtually every major truck can now be altered into a short-cab model with the sleeper in the top-mounted position, whether it be factory- or specialist-built. Basically, these normal day cabs do not leave much to be desired, but again a lot of drivers do not really fancy the idea of sleeping 'upstairs' in a claustrophobic plastic box. Especially in the early stages of development, many of these top-sleepers did not offer enough protection against heat or cold and had very little ventilation and no windows at all. After many complaints from operators who employed drivers who refused to drive these 'profit machines', most of the current equipment available can

match the majority of normal sleeper-cab accommod-ation for luxury and, in some cases surpass it, having much more living space 'up there'.

With the legal load space being so accurately de-fined in modern truck legislation, designers are really having to scratch their heads and explore every poss-ibility of utilising the very last inch of load space, be it by way of length, width, height or weight. At one time, the accent was on maximum lengths and we saw such efforts as those in the USA, where one de-sign reduced the BBC (bumper-back of cab) dimension to a meagre 21 in (53 cm)! Luckily this situation does not exist today and attention has switched to the other dimensions in an effort to get the best of what is on offer. There has always been this fight between the three facets of truck operation, with the boss, the maintenance staff and the driver all trying to get the truck which is ideal for their particular interest. The cab-top sleeper pod has proved useful in two ways because it can also act as a wind deflector where a high body line is used; otherwise a roof-mounted windshield is essential to help trim fuel costs. Early designs were naturally 'add-ons' and often definitely looked that way, while more recently the manufac-

This DAF 3300 demonstration outfit operating in homeland Netherlands, manages to combine a large cubic capacity with the ability to gross up to 50 tonnes because it has six axles.

turers of some first-line trucks, such as Volvo and DAF, have realised the potential and produced their own integrated designs. The Globetrotter and Spacecab are two such well-known designs.

Another way in which the load space can be max-imised is by closing that wasteful space between truck and trailer. The slimmer the gap, the greater the load space, but then come the problems of turning, which promotes collisions 'twixt the two units. The earliest attempts at closing that gap came about by putting a radius on the front of the trailer, thus helping with a little more load area and, at the same time, allowing the tractor unit to clear the trailer front when swing-ing round corners. This was a feature of many early Scammell matched outfits. The idea was taken a stage further by Carrimore, when they produced a semi-trailer which embodied a cruciform slot cut into the upper turntable and allowed free movement of the tractor-mounted kingpin when the outfit was turned.

In the old days of slower road speeds, not much attention was paid to wind deflection on trucks and the much publicised attempts at 'streamlining' were often aimed more at appearance and publicity rather than pure fuel saving. The gradual increase in both road speeds and the cost of fuel have forced designers to take a fresh look at what is possible to achieve in the lowering of wind drag and turbulence, thereby keeping a reasonable fuel consumption while road speeds climb further. Increasing road speeds have meant that, in addition to the general outline and head-on shape needing attention, it is the surface finish and protuberances, such as handles, mirrors and lamps, which might require smoothing out.

Returning to the load-space problem, we find that, after the initial look at ways of making sure all the linear space was taken up with the load, the next area to be tackled was across the vehicle. Over the years, there have been slight increases in overall width limits but, by and large, it has settled down to around 2.5 m or 8 ft, with variations to suit local conditions. This, in turn, has led to much juggling with unitised loads and various industries have tried to make the most of the space within the twin confines of their

With its close-coupled trailer, riding on three axles fitted with small diameter wheels, this Danish-operated TIR-tilt combination is engaged on international handling.

The coachbuilder of this Foden tractor has done his best at providing a large top-sleeper by incorporating a reverse-slope windscreen. The double-trailer outfit is engaged on long-distance removal work in Zimbabwe.

standard packaging and the overall width possible on their particular truck-body types. Vans with single-panel sides have not proved too much of a problem and, of course, the more recent curtain-sider design does allow that little bit of flexibility. It has been in temperature-controlled transport that the freighters have had to do some quiet juggling, especially if they are handling pallets and containers of varying sizes. The eventual success by some body builders with their 'thin-wall' designs has brought a sigh of relief in some quarters and the amazing results available with an insulated curtain-sided style of body has proved of great value, particularly for short-haul work.

The next direction is of course upwards and, for very many years, there were no limits set upon overall height, save that loads must be safe and not fall off. In addition, there were the more natural limitations created by overhead obstructions, varying from trees on small traffic islands to bridges and power lines in the more industrial areas. Recently, an arbitrary height of around 4 m (13 ft) has become the norm and it is this overall dimension which was the next-in-line for attention. This meant looking at ways and means of extending the load space downwards, because the upper limit was already reached by the top of the body. Therefore it was necessary to explore ways of reducing the mass needed to house the supporting

structure for the load, such as chassis frame and road wheels, together with the means to propel it along the road, such as the driveline and any other mechanical features which could not be hung elsewhere. So there is room for manoeuvre in this context.

The chassis frame to the rear of the cab is encumbered with all sorts of mechanical units necessary to the operation of the vehicle – batteries, fuel tanks, spare wheels, air reservoirs and, of course, the driveline components – historically, they have always been so placed.

One area to the rear of the cab that had received the attention of designers in the past had been that of the floor height, but usually this was in order to achieve a low load-line for ease of loading heavy items of equipment, such as tractors, crane bases, graders or very heavy lumps of industrial plant. We all know that it is possible to get the floor down to ground level for loading such items and then position it just a few inches above the road surface for transit, but this style of truck does not need to have all the units mentioned

The handsome Volvo air-cargo combination is based on the CB10M bus-chassis with underfloor-mounted 265-hp engine. With its close-coupled tandem trailer, it has all the appearance of an integrated unit, but suffers from too cramped a cab.

above located below the floor, and the road speeds of vehicles carrying such heavy items do not reach those necessary for economical long-distance freighting.

The pages of truck history are littered with ideas aimed at achieving that magical low loading-line so desired by those concerned with cutting out all the lifting necessary when manhandling heavy loads on and off. The lower the load platform the better for safety and stability but, in another respect, this is just as necessary when smaller items have to be repeatedly handled by just the driver and his mate.

Invariably, the designs for rigid low-loaders came up against the problems not only of providing storage space for all those mechanical items, but additionally of having wheels and tyres of sufficient size and capable of supporting the loads carried at everyday speeds. Faced with this problem of tyres tough enough to take the weights carried, some earlier designers just threw in the towel and mounted the rear end of the truck on solid tyres! This primitive feature, plus that of mounting the solid tyres on a dead axle

T̲he provision of a top-sleeper prevents the normal forward positioning of a refrigeration unit. This DAF combination illustrates the alternative low-slung positioning of the Carrier fridge units on both truck and trailer.

and resorting to front-wheel drive did form what can only be described as a short-term compromise. Later designers got round the problem by reducing the tyre size and adding another axle. This latter practice is still current to a degree, although recent improvements in tyre technology have eased the problems previously associated with fitting smaller diameter and smaller section tyres on high-speed trunk vehicles. The great switch to steel-braced radial tyres for trucks has improved their capabilities, while the lowering of aspect ratios has further helped the constant desire to lower load heights, which in turn provides greater load volume within the specified overall height.

Another means of providing a properly engineered, rigid low-loading chassis goes back as far as the 1930s and utilised the bus-chassis of the day. Here the main feature was the lower main-frame chassis members, which were considerably lower than their lorry counterparts which were usually engineered to correspond with loading bank height. Because the bus-chassis had to be specially formed, with an upsweep over the rear axle, combined with differing suspension and driveline layout, they were more expensive than the contemporary straight truck-type chassis frames of the day. This precluded their use except for those special vehicles, loads or customers

Specially built for woodchip hauling in Washington, USA, this big new twin-steer Freightliner with ultra-short cab and four-axle trailer can operate at a gcw of 48 tonnes. The 22.5-m (74-ft) outfit is fitted with a telescopic towbar which enables 'loading through' to be accomplished.

which could bear the higher cost, with the result that their use was by no means widespread.

Today, the bus-chassis still has its uses in truck operation, although the modern practice of chassis-less construction did preclude the use of certain designs in days gone by. Nevertheless, as mentioned above, both Volvo and DAF passenger-chassis have been used for special applications where the additional cost of the more specialised coach-chassis is more than offset by the value of the traffic handled.

Even greater refinement has been achieved by a handful of specialist builders, including Terberg, Rolfo, Titan, Kassbohrer and Ginaf, who have produced interesting practical designs embodying a fair proportion of current truck-production components. By utilising many standard parts, such as cabs, engines, transmissions and axles, and then adding such special 'one-off' parts as required, the initial cost is kept to a reasonable level and future parts required during routine servicing are largely available through normal manufacturers' agents and dealers.

Rolfo of Italy naturally use the Iveco chassis as the starting point of their high-capacity conversions and

a typical outfit is a 6 × 4 low-loading chassis based on the Iveco 190.38 model but equipped with 22.5 in wheels on the single front axle and 19.5 in wheels on the two rear axles. An additional factor, aimed at gaining a few vital centimetres in the height available for load space, is to specify low aspect-ratio tyres for the outfit, these being 315/80R22.5 at the front and 265/70R19.5 at the rear.

Overall, the trailer combination is 18 m (59 ft) long and 4 m (13 ft) high, with a gross weight of 24 tonnes solo and 44 tonnes with trailer. Total volume is 115 m³ (150 yd³).

Terberg in the Netherlands have also produced a machine somewhat similar to that mentioned above, except that the overall cube capacity has been increased by the provision of an overcab extension to the body. Unladen weight has been kept down by using a 6 × 2 layout and, with a 233 hp Volvo T100A engine and three-axle trailer, the whole being mounted on 15-in wheels, the gross weight is just under 41 tonnes.

Similarly, in West Germany, the specialist truck-builder Titan, which has been in the forefront of many revolutionary designs over the past few years, has chosen a 4 × 2 front-wheel drive layout. Working in collaboration with the old established body builder Kassbohrer, the MAN-cabbed outfit manages to come up with an incredible 760-mm (30-in) chassis height, thus providing over 3 m (9 ft 10 in) available for those bulky cargoes.

A totally new vehicle concept was introduced in 1984 by the West German company of Steinwinter, in co-operation with Daimler-Benz, Drogmoller and Schmitz. Instead of positioning only the mechanical driveline beneath the freight deck, the Steinwinter team of engineers came up with a design whereby the complete very low-profile tractor unit sits entirely under the 18 m (59 ft) long semi-trailer. This new concept, shown as a prototype during the Internationale Automobil-Ausstellung show in Frankfurt, is powered by a 375-hp Mercedes OM422 diesel and rides on five axles, of which three are steerable and most air-suspended. The huge trailer can be positioned up to a loading deck from either front or rear, which helps speed up cargo handling tremendously.

This unique contraption has, since its introduction, also been manufactured as a rigid chassis, pulling a drawbar trailer and hauling two large containers, but it remains to be seen if either design gets into regular use. Although the low aerodynamic cab resembles that of the most fancy sports car, with its leather interior, neat sporty instrumentation and classy bucket seats, not many truck drivers are prepared to duck down there underneath a 20 tonne load.

Years ago, the giant Strick Corporation in the USA developed a project of low-profile tractor which was of such low height as to be coupled under its series of interchangeable bodies, but, due to the powerful transport union interferences, the revolutionary idea was never allowed to proceed. This interesting con-

The space-age design of the German Steinwinter super-volume tractor/semi-trailer outfit offers many advantages, but drivers are not impressed with the idea of sitting so close to the crumple zone!

cept was doomed before serious manufacture could be contemplated and no driver wanted to run it.

Other notable low-cab designs include the Bussing Decklaster, which was actually designed for handling a system of small containers carried on rails, and the Foden, which was really a carry-over of the crane-carrier chassis, where a low cab is useful to keep the crane jib almost level in transit. Only time will tell if the Steinwinter will ever be successful on the roads of Europe, coming as it does after other designs have failed to make an impression. Perhaps times have changed now for the better, for among all the mundane trucks on the highways there now and again appears something that seems to be a pointer for the future. Our new trucks seem to be breaking the mould of what has gone before and several late designs are definitely much more slick than a few years back. A look at some of the present-day touring coaches indicates what could very soon follow in the truck world to improve productivity and efficiency still further.

Of course, it would be ideal if a vehicle combination consisted only of usable load space, but the mechanicals and driving compartment have to be included in

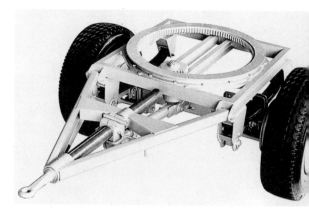

lose-up view of the front-axle/turntable assembly of the PAL system by Joseph Peitz. Note the small gear-wheel inside the turntable ring gear which extends the drawbar on tight turns.

the overall design. Furthermore, there are a great number of legal requirements relating to the size, construction and use of trucks which also limit the total load space available.

Over the last 10 years, much pioneering work has been done by both operators themselves and the body-building industry and many innovative ideas have been worked out successfully. Of special interest is the close-coupling of trailers, which has offered substantial gains in cubic capacity, and the gap which used to be at least 150 cm (5 ft) has been reduced to an amazing 20 cm (8 in) in some instances. Automatic trailer couplings located far forward under the lead-truck chassis are generally applied now in many countries and, for higher weight running, double drawbars have become more popular than before. Although this construction method does not gain as much space as the under-chassis frame coupling, it can still save up to 1 m (3¼ ft) compared with normal hook-ups. A third system is the trombone: when the combination is being driven in a straight line on the road, it is close-coupled whereas, when manoeuvring, the distance between truck and trailer can be lengthened.

The basic design feature of the close-coupled trailer system is the inclusion of a means whereby the drawbar coupling between truck and trailer is capable of automatic variation to suit the relative positions of the two units. Therefore the prime requisite is that the coupling is closed up to its shortest for straight-ahead running and yet extends automatically to maintain a safe distance between the two units when the occasion arises because of turns or manoeuvring.

In the PAL system by Josef Peitz of West Germany, the required movement is achieved by having an internal ring gear on the trailer turntable. Meshing with this ring gear is a small pinion located on the end of a small crank pivoted to the extending drawbar rod. In practice, as the A-frame of the drawbar is turned into a curve, so the ring gear rotates, causing the gear-

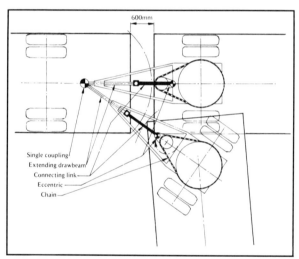

Single coupling
Extending drawbeam
Connecting link
Eccentric
Chain

600mm

iagram which serves to illustrate the operation of the Dutch Contar system whereby the sliding drawbar extends on tight turns to maintain sufficient clearance between truck and trailer.

wheel to revolve, which turns the crank arm and pushes out the sliding drawbar, so lengthening the space between truck and trailer. With the drawbar at an angle of 39°, the maximum increase of drawbar length is 60 cm (23½ in).

Much the same result is obtained with the Contar system produced by the Dutch company of the same name. This design uses a sliding tube as the drawbar and, in use, it is pushed out by the action of a small turntable and eccentric pivot pin which are chain-driven by the main trailer turntable. As the trailer is taken out of the straight-ahead line, the endless chain which is tight around the periphery of the trailer turntable rotates the smaller turntable, moving the eccentric pin towards the towing vehicle and pushing out the drawbar, so increasing the gap between the two units. A minimum distance of 60 cm (23½ in) is possible without truck and trailer colliding.

The West German firm of Orthaus uses a different technique in that a diagonal link is provided between the trailer turntable and a special V-shaped towbar which in turn is attached to the normal truck-coupling jaw through a special well-braced tube arrangement aimed at keeping the drawbar rigid and in line with the truck. The design calls for all movement between truck and trailer to take place *via* the diagonal members, which provide something similar to Ackermann steering geometry. A hinged bar is provided so that the diagonal steering bars can be locked in the straight-ahead position.

Until now, Ackermann-Fruehauf have produced probably the best-matched outfits embodying the high-volume close-coupled concept. Rather surprisingly, this combination is operated by the Hungarian State transport organisation.

Engaged on international removals is this DAF 2100 with close-coupled tandem-van-trailer, both with Sparshatt bodywork embodying custom-built canopy-side loading. The long trailer-hitch is on the truck's rear axle for minimum swing when turning.

Ackermann-Fruehauf of Wuppertal – home of the historic overhead railway – have produced two variations of their GLZ system, for although the original GLZ name was applied to the complete close-coupled outfit mentioned earlier, it is also used for their equipment aimed at reducing that wasteful gap.

One type of coupling uses a long single-drawbar arm and employs a single trailer turntable with a pivot forward of the actual turntable locating on the drawbar. A limit stop is incorporated to prevent the trailer turning at more than about 45°, but for yard manoeuvring the drawbar can be extended and locked in position so that it then handles like a conventional trailer coupling.

The second type in the GLZ system employs two turntables with an adaptor frame positioned between them. One long drawbar beam is fixed to the normal trailer hitch on the truck and is pivoted just in front of the lower turntable. This drawbar is telescopic and steers the trailer turntable and bogie. The adaptor frame also has a shorter drawbar A-frame, which is

pivoted short of the main trailer hitch and is limited in its swinging arc by means of the special swivel stop. This hefty fabrication is arranged at the rear of the truck and can be swung down out of the way if it is necessary to tow trailers with the old type of swinging A-frame drawbars.

Although the drawbar combinations appear to be grabbing all the action during the past few years, the common tractor/semi-trailer outfit has also gained considerably in load space due to the employment of top-sleepers on tractor units and an increase in the length of semi-trailers to around 13.75 m (45 ft) within the 15.5 m (50 ft 10 in) overall. Again these far more productive machines are not exclusively for low-weight bulky goods but, depending on local axle-capacity regulations, can easily load up to a maximum gcw of 38 tonnes or more.

All these 'new generation' trucks are giving operators the chance to maximise the payload of their equipment, but unfortunately this type of specialised transport has not been possible everywhere. Notably the Scandinavian countries have faced some problems in employing vehicles with sleeper boxes mounted on the cab roof which cannot meet the very stringent safety requirements of the Swedish law-makers relating to cab strength and, in particular, the downward blow to the roof.

However, the recently introduced modified Globetrotter shortcab by Volvo – the 'Eurotrotter' – offers two sleeping berths and a very well appointed interior layout. The large Swedish furniture producer, Kinnarps, has been operating a prototype F10 with the new arrangement, coupled to twin box-van trailers, and 32.5 cm (82½ in) in load space has been gained by using the new cab. Sweden has always been Europe's most liberal country when it comes to vehicle measurements and weights, allowing massive 52-tonne combinations to reach up to 24 m (78¾ ft) in length, and understandably there never has been as much pressure to operate top high-cube vehicles as in other countries which suffer far more restrictive regulations. But with competition being so keen, even haulers operating at such generous weights and lengths still try to cram in as much freight as possible in order to earn that extra dollar – or kroner.

The world of parcels carriers has probably seen as much change in recent years as most other areas of transport operation, with some of the old established parcels carriers having to change their ways or go into other traffics in order to stay alive. The parcels traffic can be full of variables for often no two items are the same, whether it be shape, weight or size. While some carriers will accept almost anything, so long as it can be loaded into the van, other operators

By the adoption of similar-sized wheels and tyres throughout, a uniform floor height and overall appearance is possible. The close-coupled tandem-trailer will track closely when turning, but is not so stable as a conventional drawbar at high speeds.

are more selective and items such as heavy rolls of carpet will only be carried at a premium! In particular it is the speed of the parcels-carriers operations which have seen the greatest change and everything they do is aimed at maintaining the very tight trunk-route schedules which are essential if they are to stay ahead of the competition.

One operator which stands out in this near-revolution of the parcels world is TNT-Ipec. In order to make its already smooth express operation in Sweden more efficient, it has taken delivery of a fascinating 'road train' produced by Scania and Kalmar-Lagab. This combination consists of a long-wheelbase 142M 6 × 2 tractor and a long widespread tandem semi-trailer plus a second close-coupled bogie trailer; it is capable of transporting no less than three full-size 7.15 m (23½ ft) demountable containers, all within an overall length limit of 24 m (78¾ ft). This is achieved by utilising an hydraulic trombone system on the rearmost drawbar trailer, as seen on many other European high-volume outfits. When driven straight,

This DAF 2100-hauled drawbar outfit by Joseph Peitz clearly illustrates the close-coupling possible by the use of the company's PAL system. Maximum trailer cube is assured by the use of small wheels.

it is tight up to the lead semi-trailer, but when cornering the gap widens automatically. This outfit shows just what can be obtained by careful design and planning in order to exploit the regulations to the full.

Looking outside Europe, there seems to be far less need for such sophisticated machinery, taking advantage of every cubic centimetre allowed, but then it has all to start somewhere, In the USA, where some feel that 'trucking' was born, it is noticeable that not much has been done in this field and only on the West Coast, where legislation is more liberal, have some truly high-volume combinations appeared in recent years.

A number of operators there are running tri-axle rigid trucks, pulling big two-axle drawbars with large box-van bodies, mainly between the states of California, Oregon and Washington or up into western Canada. These outfits are based on very short-cabbed Freightliner and Peterbilt trucks, mostly with day cabs, but the hook-up between truck and trailer works on a similar principle to the European offerings, though a combination of under-chassis frame coupling and hydraulic trombone-type towbar is also used. Many of these big rigs also have facilities for loading-through, enabling both units to be loaded and unloaded without the need to unhitch the trailer.

Custom-built designs to achieve the utmost in vehicle efficiency have been around in many countries but never to the extent that they are today and, of course, development is still going on. All this activity is good for the manufacturers of the equipment and, in turn, the operators, for transport is still very much a cut-throat business. Let us hope that, in the struggle for higher efficiency by all connected with the trucking industry, the lonely guy up front is remembered, for he is still the most important investment of all.

MULTI-TRAILER COMBINATIONS

Although two and even three trailers may be pulled behind a tractor unit in some parts of the world nowadays, the 'double' or 'triple' rig is most often associated with the USA. It is in the USA that twin- and triple-trailer hook-ups are most often seen on the regular road network and, although not allowed in every state, these impressive combinations have found acceptance with many companies and state authorities across the nation.

It certainly seems likely that multiple-trailer rigs had their origins in the USA since there are many records of twin- and even triple-trailer combinations operating as early as the 1920s. These monsters had quickly found their way into some fleets for the obvious reason that their productivity was amazingly good, but driver comfort and top speeds were less impressive. Motive power was provided by vehicles such as chain-drive Macks and it was not unusual for the entire rig, or at least the trailers, to be equipped with solid tyres. And because the Motor Carriers Act of 1935 was still a long way off, 'luxuries' such as rearview mirrors and clearance lights were omitted from the specification. For the intrepid private motorist in a small car, or the driver of a horsedrawn vehicle, encountering one of these triple-trailer combinations must have been a mind-boggling experience, particularly at night!

Recent years have witnessed an increasing acceptance of multi-trailer rigs as their reputation for safety and overall productivity has spread from west to east. The standard triple is a 26- or 27-ft (7.9–8.2-metre) van while doubles can stretch to 42- or even 45-footers (12.8 to 13.7 m). Operation of these leviathans is confined to interstates, divided highways, turnpikes and other similar roads, although

some states permit limited access to ordinary, undivided routes.

Restrictions governing twin- or triple-trailer operation are necessary, primarily for reasons of space for, in the same way as the huge Road Trains used in Australia's outback would not be suitable for the congested centres of cities such as London or Paris, multi-trailer rigs don't suit every area of the USA. This presents problems for truckers wishing to cross from one state to another, or even needing to leave the designated routes on which doubles or triples can be used. As a result, those states which do allow such rigs have parking areas at their borders where trains may be broken down and trailers hooked up individually to a short-haul tractor for the completion of the journey.

Travel any of the routes permitting twin- or triple-trailer combinations and you will inevitably come across a rig stranded on the hard shoulder, the telltale smell of a burnt-out clutch wafting on the breeze. Or perhaps on a road such as the New York to Buffalo thruway you will overtake a twin 42-ft (12.8-m) trailer doubles rig and catch the driver slouched back in his seat, one foot up on the dashboard! For these drivers, the regular run from one end of a concrete ribbon to the other must indeed be a monotonous task, despite the size of the rig which they are driving. The tractors too are lower geared than the normal highway job, to allow for the higher weights, so forget about 'getting the lights' from the regular driver of a doubles rig if you are trucking on by in your 450 Cat-powered KW eighteen-wheeler. It's not that they are ignorant of the rules of the road, just that they are always being passed and life in the slow lane is never much fun!

For reasons of compatibility, the 'standard' hook-

Volvo F12 double in the Netherlands operating on a good stretch of highway linking two main routes which are motor roads. Twin tanks are most often used for these unusual combinations.

up for multi-trailer rigs comprises a coupling on the rear of the lead trailer to which is hooked a single- or twin-axle 'dolly' by means of a pin or pintlehook. The dolly itself has a fifth wheel coupling sitting atop the axle(s) and this in turn accepts the kingpin of another semi-trailer. This hook-up may be continued *ad infinitum*, or at least until the combination reaches its maximum legal length.

This method of making up a multi-trailer rig has the advantage already mentioned of allowing any type of semi-trailer to be coupled to the dolly (or converter-dolly as it is sometimes known) but, in terms of stability, the arrangement has definite limitations. The problem is simply that two pivot points (pintlehook and kingpin) permit excessive movement and this is exaggerated with each hook-up of another

trailer. The result is often quite erratic wandering by the second or third trailer under certain conditions and this movement, once started, is completely outside the control of the driver. The American Federal Highway Administration (FHWA) report on doubles operation, published in 1985, states that the 'off-tracking characteristics of doubles is about twice that of a single trailer rig' and that this 'may contribute to the large number of rollover accidents at tight loop ramps (highway interchanges) where high-speed off-tracking can cause the rear trailer tyres to hit a kerb, thus precipitating a blow out'.

Another problem, only recently overcome, concerned brake imbalance since, on a multi-trailer rig, retardation should ideally start from the rearmost axle and work forward. Such sophistication,

Mercedes-Benz enjoy a unique position in South Africa in that their engines are the only ones approved for use in heavy trucks. This beautiful 6 × 4 tractor and doubles rig is seen in the semi-plus-pup configuration.

pioneered in Australia, has only recently been adopted by North American brake-system manufacturers and earlier types were less than ideal in terms of response times and balance. However, according to the FHWA, modern doubles 'appear to respond to braking as well as singles' and 'safety is expected to be improved by the new design of dollies' so drivers of these big rigs can look forward to an easier life in future.

A series of spectacular accidents in Michigan during the late 1970s resulted in the famous 'Michigan Train' tank doubles being banned from the centre of all large urban areas. In this case, it was not only the behaviour of the second trailer which was causing difficulties, but the overall height of the tanks. This

combination of a very high centre of gravity and less than ideal handling made rollover accidents almost inevitable, regardless of the skill of the driver and, although undeniably very efficient in terms of the amount of payload that could be hauled, the rigs were an obvious hazard in the wrong environment.

Today Michigan tank doubles are restricted to an overall height of 11 ft 8½ in (3.6 m) and their operation is limited to certain routes between the hours of midnight and 6 a.m. in counties having a population in excess of 600,000. This legislation governs all inflammable liquids with a flash point lower than 70°F (21°C) and has been successful in reducing the number of fires resulting from rollover incidents to almost nil.

Efforts to improve the handling of twin-tank combinations first saw fundamental changes to their design in Canada. The new combination was to become known as a B-train and the main difference between it and its predecessor was in the important area of the hook-up between the first and second trailer.

Remarkable for many reasons is this exquisite B-train rig used by Fleetham Cartage in British Columbia. Hauled by a Western Star cabover tractor (built by Volvo-White) and powered by a 475-hp Cummins, the rig comprises two 'platypus' dual-purpose trailers capable of hauling deck loads in one direction and liquid resin in low-slung tanks on the return journey.

The B-train eliminated the pintlehook and divider dolly entirely and substituted a short tail on the lead trailer onto which a fifth wheel coupling was installed. By removing one pivot point in this way, the overall handling of the combination was dramatically improved, some drivers even claiming that these huge rigs could be reversed once a bit of experience had been gained. But of course the vital ingredient, 'interchangeability', of the trailers was also removed, since the rearmost trailer of a B-train rig did not carry a fifth wheel on its back end.

Today most of Canada's big doubles combinations are B-trains and these are used to haul commodities ranging from bricks to dressed timber and glue to grain. Most able to benefit from the introduction of these safer, yet bigger rigs, were the oil companies and it is in the tank-truck sector of the industry that the B-train has enjoyed its biggest success.

Most of these rigs are immediately distinguishable from their A-train brethren, but one exception is found in Canada's western seaboard province, British

Columbia. In this area, the tandem-axle assembly at the rear of the lead trailer is located immediately underneath the tail section. This has the beneficial effect of giving excellent weight distribution but the rig certainly looks for all the world like an earlier A-train. Not that the drivers of these huge and cleverly designed rigs worry too much about the confusing appearance of axle layouts. Far more important to them is the number of polished chrome items on their tractors, or the power of the diesels needed to pull them over the Rocky Mountains. In both areas the drivers are fortunate indeed since British Columbia not only has a power-to-weight ratio which results in most doubles rigs having at least 440 hp, but British Columbian truckers are among the most appearance-

Operating under special authority in Hamilton, Ontario, this Paystar 5000 doubles rig hauls no less than six 15-ton coils of steel from one plant to another *via* public highways. Speed is restricted to 24 km/h (15 mph) and truck specifications are heavy duty all the way.

Although doubles combinations are generally regarded as being heavy units, they are often used to haul lightweight 'balloon' freight. In the USA, Volvo-White are marketing the European Volvo F7 range as a lightweight tractor suitable for hauling highway doubles on balloon freight.

conscious in Canada, so chrome goodies, marker lights and attractive paint schemes are found in abundance.

Despite the obvious advantages of the B-train, the conventional pintlehook/converter-dolly set-up (now called an A-train) is still used, this system being preferred for triple combinations, such as those operated by Soo-Security on designated highways in Canada's mid-western provinces. In such instances, the versatility of the older system makes it more cost effective than the newer B-train, despite the infinitely better handling of the latter.

Another country concerned with the safety of twin-trailer combinations is Sweden, which although allowing such rigs, restricted their operation to a maximum speed of 40 km/h (25 mph)! until early 1986, when the limit was raised to 70 km/h (44 mph).

Sweden's government is one which recognises the valuable contribution made to its economy by its road-transport industry and, generally speaking, introduces legislation which does not completely hog-tie its truckers. Length and weight limits are the highest anywhere in Europe or Scandinavia, but the rules in force there favour the operation of truck-trailer combinations and 'doubles' are used by only a few companies.

Of these, perhaps the best known is the furniture-maker, Kinnarps, which runs twin box-van semi-trailers behind Volvo Globetrotter tractors. This operation is unique, however, in that Kinnarps has enjoyed special authority to run its doubles at the normal maximum highway speed for trucks of 70 km/h (44 mph). The company started its doubles operations 17 years ago, at which time speed limits for all types of truck were set at 40 km/h (25 mph), and in a period which saw a fair number of doubles on Sweden's highways. But when the limit was raised to 70 km/h (44 mph) for all combinations except doubles, these almost entirely disappeared from the scene and it was only the unblemished safety record of the Kinnarps vehicles that convinced the authorities to allow their operation at normal highway speeds.

Needless to say, those companies which could benefit from the use of doubles made strong representation to the government throughout the 1970s and 1980s in order to get the limit raised from its restrictive 40-km/h (25-mph) level. To date, however, the government has remained largely unimpressed, although, in 1984, they did monitor an experiment handled by a number of Swedish truck-, trailer- and equipment-manufacturers to discover ways of improving the handling of A-train-style doubles. Designated 'Projekt Dubbel', the experiments centred around a new type of VBG drawbar coupling which locked out at highway speeds in order to eliminate the tendency of the second trailer to wander off course. Speed sensors located on the semi-trailer axles determined at what speed the first and second trailers should be locked together and also controlled the braking effort at each axle in the eight-axle combination.

Results of the test indicate that such a system is

effective but, unfortunately, it is also expensive and, in any case, the Swedish authorities have not blessed it with their official seal of approval.

Truck-trailer combinations are probably more common throughout Europe than the tractor-semi-trailer or artic, but it is only in the Netherlands that one can find genuine doubles in operation.

These appear to be exclusively bulk-tank units and most examples are hauled behind DAF tractors. Over-all length for these doubles is restricted to 18 m (59 ft) so there is not a great deal of room in which to exploit the advantages offered by two trailers. What the doubles do offer the Dutch operator is flexibility, although in recent years this has been curtailed some-what by the introduction of new legislation confining doubles to specified routes. The problem, as with the big doubles in Michigan, was that a few accidents involving these rigs were enough to convince the authorities that they were inherently unsafe. There was talk at one stage of banning their use altogether, but a compromise was finally arrived at whereby doubles could operate only on designated routes, and safety inspections by the Dutch Transport Depart-ment were stepped up considerably. Particular atten-tion is paid to the dolly which is correctly pinpointed as being the obvious source of problems but, apart from that, the doubles operator has little more to fear from the 'ministry man' than any other trucker.

Today, permits for doubles can still be obtained, although operators wishing to get into this type of rig for the first time will experience resistance from several sources. The technical specification of the en-tire combination (i.e. tractor and trailers) has to be checked and approved by the authorities before an

Bottom-hopper trailers used for bulk loads of grain or fertilizer are interestingly designed as illustrated by this doubles rig hauled by an immaculate Peterbilt 362-series tractor unit.

application for the doubles permit will even be consi-dered, so truckers hoping to pull a 'Road Train' in the Netherlands have to be sure that they have done their sums correctly from the very beginning.

The term 'road train' is often applied to doubles and triples and sometimes even to a rigid truck hauling a single drawbar trailer, but the *real* trains have their home in the desolate Australian outback.

These giant rigs really are trains, stretching up to an incredible 49 m (160 ft) in length overall and grossing up to 107.5 tonnes. And these are just the artics! Rigid 4-axle trucks hauling three full trailers can reach even greater dimensions, the largest snaking out over a serpentine 60 m (197 ft) and grossing 124.5 tonnes!

To the average trucker, such rigs defy the imagin-ation, and the very idea of pulling out of a depot at the start of a thousand-mile (1,600-km) run across the wastes of Western Aussie at the wheel of a growling Mack or high-rise KW is the sort of thing of which dreams are made. But the reality is very different. The terrain crossed by what are probably the biggest trucks in the world is tough on both drivers and equipment and there is little hope of survival for either the inexperienced or the under-specified.

Many colourful and exciting stories surround the road trains of Australia and the breed of hard-working and resourceful men who drive them. True, the one thing they don't have to contend with is

I̶n̶ New Zealand, doubles are often used and are referred to as 'Canadian-style' when used in the B-train mode. This Kenworth K-100 6 × 4 unit and B-train make an impressive sight.

traffic. In fact, in the more desolate areas, truckers get really excited if they meet another half-dozen rigs over 500 miles (800 km). But although they are not likely to be worrying about clipping the front end of a badly parked Volkswagen in a busy downtown street, they are concerned equally about the state of the weather and its effect on the dirt roads which make up a large part of the road-train's routes. Swirling red bulldust which finds its way into man and machine is part of the pleasure of dry weather, while the rains have the unwelcome ability to wash out bridges and sections of road in a few short hours. Add to these hazards, the equally unwelcome prospects of changing several tyres and (if you are lucky) just missing a belligerent bullock or kamikaze kangaroo, and it is soon apparent that the average road-train haul is no milk run. Perhaps all that is certain about these machines and their dedicated drivers is that, without them, whole communities would perish and disappear from view. It is a case of essential supplies in and raw materials out and the economy of those areas served by road trains would never be viable without them.

At one time, it was British trucks which powered Australia's biggest rigs and marques such as Atkinson, Foden, Scammell and AEC ruled the roost. In recent years, the position has changed in favour of the top-flight Americans. Kenworth, Mack, International and White now dominate the scene, although Scania, Volvo, Mercedes and Nissan are all making a concerted effort to make their presence felt in this small, yet prestigious sector of the market.

At least part of the reason behind the decline of the British heavy in Australia and the subsequent rise of the Americans rests with the ability of the latter to build exactly the specification required to suit a particular job. This is evidenced by the fact that those European and Swedish truck builders anxious to fight it out with the North Americans are offering components such as Rockwell axles, Fuller transmissions, Hendrickson suspension systems and Spicer clutches as special options to suit road-train work, a tacit acknowledgement that their own components are not quite up to par for such gruelling hauls. The resulting hybrid Europeans are not to be underestimated

Linking major cities in Canada is a high-speed service offering delivery times competitive with air freight even over long distances. Tractor is an International 4070 and trailers are 8.2-m (27-ft) Ram units.

though, and both Mercedes and Scania claim that their own engines regularly return better fuel figures than the big Cummins and Detroit lumps fitted in the American tractors.

For road-train operators, however, it is not so much a question of economy as one of durability. For while it may well be a tremendous advantage to have an engine capable of returning very good fuel figures, it is of little use to the operator if the truck in which it is installed shakes itself apart on its third trip across the Nullabor Plains!

Kenworth were quick to acknowledge this fact and responded by designing a truck specifically for the Australian market. Designated the SAR, this big unit retained the aggressive good looks of the conventional KW, but incorporated some features that made it particularly suitable for road-train work.

In the first place, the cab was raised to a position well above the height of a 900 series, which meant that the crew enjoyed improved forward visibility and were up above the dust kicked up by other traffic using the dirt roads. Another benefit was that long-distance fuel tanks could be installed along almost the entire length of the chassis, a bonus on most operations but an absolute necessity for road-train units.

The standard engine when the SAR was first introduced was the Cummins KT-450 but, as the truck has gained popularity, so the list of available driveline components has grown to meet all requirements. The success of the SAR, easily distinguished from all other Kenworths by its distinctive sloping bonnet or hood, has not yet encouraged other manufacturers to build an Australian 'special', but at least some of the Europeans are going part of the way by introducing OEM components to trucks normally built entirely in-house.

Still in the southern hemisphere, we find that neighbouring New Zealand, although not allowing multi-trailer trains, does permit A- and B-trains on its normal highway system.

What the Kiwi rigs lack in terms of sheer size is more than compensated for by the stylish way in which they are decorated. Not only does the New Zealand trucker rejoice in eye-catching paint

In addition to knowing how to handle cattle, drivers of livestock vehicles must be able to operate smoothly in order to keep their charges on their feet. Such a task is not always easy as can be seen from this picture of a Road Train fording a small stream in Western Australia.

schemes, but other 'down-under' items, such as bull-bars, stone-guards and marine lights, also find their way on to trucks which seldom leave a hard-surfaced highway. New Zealand is also more cosmopolitan than Australia in terms of the number of truck manufacturers represented there and rare models, such as Oshkosh and Pacific, share the beautiful landscape with ERFs and Leylands, as well as the now universal Volvo, Scania, Kenworth and International heavies.

Doubles outfits in New Zealand normally run on seven axles and the most common configuration is a three-axle tractor hauling two tandem-axle semi-trailers, either in B-train style or in the older, and more commonplace, semi-plus-pup layout. Another popular combination is the rigid eight-wheeler, hauling either three- or four-axle full trailers. These are particularly popular with operators hauling timber or livestock, although other commodities are moved in these impressive machines.

Although conservative when measured against the mighty Australian outback road trains, New

Zealand's twin-trailer combinations operate at a practical 39-tonnes gross and within a 19-m (62 ft 4 in) overall length limit. Obviously tare weights are important and manufacturers there regard weight savings as a very high priority but, as in Switzerland, weight paring is not done at the expense of longevity and even among the already heavy trucks, such as Volvo and Scania, components such as Hendrickson beam suspensions and Malco spoke wheels are listed as options. Meanwhile, lighter vehicles, such as ERF and Foden, enjoy a considerable advantage over their Swedish competitors in this area. However, in the over 20-tonne gvw stakes, the European builders do not fare well at all. Four of the top six bestsellers are Japanese, while International and Mack take the other top spots and only Mercedes and Volvo achieve anything like the sort of volume necessary to maintain a profitable position in the marketplace.

In South Africa we find not only an efficient and modern road-transport industry but also twin-trailer combinations which have been in use since the early 1960s.

The most commonly-used combination has always

In Michigan, the maximum legal gross for a 'train' is 70 tonnes. Trucks are worked hard as evidenced by this tired Kenworth cabover hauling two dump trailers.

been a 6 × 4 tractor unit (rather quaintly referred to, even today, as a 'horse' or mechanical horse) coupled to a 10- or 11-m (32 ft 10 in–36 ft) semi-trailer; this in turn tows a short, two-axle 'pup' trailer. Popular since the days when high-powered 6 × 4 tractors first hit the market there, these interesting rigs are still found today in some numbers although, as in Australia, tractor units are more likely to be American or European than British. Certainly Foden, Leyland and ERF still maintain a presence, but gone are the days that once saw these units, often with locally built cabs, moving the really heavyweight commodities.

Legislation governing axle weights, lengths and gross combination weights in South Africa is tough indeed and working out the best vehicle for a given job requires a deal of knowledge and the use of a complicated formula relating to the distance between the centreline of the outermost axles. Although few combinations can actually achieve the maximum, in theory at least, a gross combination weight of 50.2 tonnes within an overall length of 20 m (about 65$\frac{1}{2}$ ft) is possible. In practice, 48 tonnes is more realistic and this applies equally to the traditional seven-axle 'semi-plus-pup' combination and the much newer 'interlink' system.

Interlink is the name given to the system pioneered in Canada and known there as the B-train. In South Africa, credit for the introduction of the undoubtably efficient twin-trailer rig goes to Henred-Fruehauf who first hit the road with a prototype in 1980. Since that time, the Interlink has been slowly replacing the older semi-plus-pup, as the older equipment wears out. The advantages for this type of hook-up have already been explained and the obvious benefits are as welcome in the bottom part of Africa as in the top half of North America.

Pioneer of the genuine American-style double in South Africa, however, was Stuttafords Van Lines, a Cape-Town-based furniture hauler which favoured 4 × 2 Oshkosh E-series tractors hauling twin vans from the mid 1960s until 1983 when the South African distributor for this marque closed its doors.

Stuttafords were quick to realise the advantages offered by employing two identical single-axle semi-trailers on their type of work where cubic capacity and not weight is the important factor. South Africa is a huge country and its large industrial and commercial centres are separated by vast distances. It made sense to load two vans with household effects at separate locations in the same area and then to couple them together for the long haul.

But there was another reason too. In the 1960s, the maximum overall length of vehicles was reduced from 72 ft to 65 ft (21.9 to 19.8 m) while at the same time overall height was increased from 12 ft 6 in to 13 ft (3.8 to 4 m). In order not to lose volume, Stuttafords and Fruehauf put their heads together and the first South African double was born.

As pioneers of this system, the company was naturally in the limelight so Stuttafords ensured that their rigs were made as safe as possible. Hope anti-jackknife devices were installed on all units and crews were specially trained not only in how to move household goods, but also how to operate their sophisticated new vehicles. Today, Stuttafords operate 700 vehicles and Mercedes 4 × 2 tractors have replaced the Oshkosh. But doubles are still utilised wherever possible and Stuttafords are a regular sight on the highways of South Africa.

A particularly interesting development of the twin-trailer arrangement in South Africa concerns a combination of European and American technology. Several operators now employ modern B-train doubles, not only on platform and tank work but also on jobs requiring the use of curtain-sider trailers. Curtain-siders are enormously popular throughout Europe, but have been slow to catch on in the USA, operators there claiming that extreme weather conditions would bring about unacceptably rapid deterioration of their equipment. This situation is changing a little as some companies cautiously feel out the system for certain applications (the Allegheny Bottling Company uses 46 ft (14 m) long 'Beverage-liner' semi-trailers behind Mack tractors to haul Pepsi-Cola) but box-vans are still very much the order of the day.

By way of contrast, South Africa has no such problems and operators there are in the fortunate position of being able to take full advantage of the most

Limited numbers of doubles are operated in the Netherlands on specified routes. The vehicles are limited to a maximum overall length of 18 m (59 ft) and are generally tank trailers.

modern techniques and equipment from both worlds.

It is easy for Westerners to assume that, with the possible exception of mineral-rich South Africa, very little serious heavy-duty trucking takes place throughout the remainder of the whole vast African continent. Little could be farther from the truth. In point of fact, Zimbabwe, itself an area more than three times the size of England, boasts a modern and efficient road transport industry evidenced by a generous 55-tonne gcw and a variety of interesting if unusual heavy vehicles.

AVM is not a name familiar to most of us, yet the manufacturer of the truck that carries this name, W. Dahmer & Company, claims a capacity of some 1,500 trucks a year. While this is not exactly earth-shattering, it can be put into context by remembering that Foden produce around half that number each year.

First formed in 1957, Dahmer started building trucks in 1960, having managed to secure the franchise for DAF vehicles. In the early days, AVMs were virtually 100% DAF and, as such, were almost indistinguishable from the original product but, by the mid 1970s, almost every component, apart from the driveline, was built by Dahmer. Today a range of trucks from around 10 tonnes gvw to 70 tonnes gcw is produced at the factory in Harare and the finished product bears only a passing resemblance to its Dutch cousin.

Until recently, AVM vehicles were equipped with a fixed cab (the original having been modelled on the fixed cab 2600 series DAF) but an all-new AVM-designed tilt cab was introduced in 1984. Another recent, and surprising, innovation is the roof-mounted sleeper pod, a feature now commonplace on European trucks but not generally associated with African vehicles.

Engines from 116 to 330 hp are used in a variety of chassis, all of which are tailored to local requirements. Largest unit is the CD-718, a 6 × 4 tractor unit powered by the familiar 330-hp DAF diesel. Suspension systems using rubber springs or dampers are not unknown in Europe, at least on the rear axle or axles, but the AVM goes one better by making a rubber system standard fitting on both the front and rear axles. Advantages claimed are resistance to corrosion and a completely maintenance-free system.

A maximum gross weight of 55 tonnes is possible throughout Zimbabwe using either the tractor-trailer plus pup concept or the more modern interlink twin semi-system which spilled over into the country from neighbouring South Africa. Maximum overall length is a generous 22 m (72 ft 2 in) for tractor-trailer combinations. For some reason a limit of 44 tonnes is put on truck-trailer rigs but, conversely, there is a more generous length limit and as many as three trailers may be hauled, provided the maximum permitted gtw is not exceeded.

The appearance of the AVM cannot be said to be ultra-modern but truck operators in Zimbabwe are concerned more about reliability and ruggedness than about fancy good looks. That having been said, the no frills appearance of the truck and its individuality combine to give the truck an appeal of its own. Zimbabwe is a long haul from the flat, modern Netherlands and today's AVM is many a mile from the DAF product on which it was based.

One undoubted drawback of the conventional doubles hook-up is the redundancy of the converter-dolly once the train is broken down and the separate trailers coupled to individual tractor units.

Recognising this, Ackermann-Fruehauf (A-F), a German manufacturer of trailers and allied equipment, recently introduced the prototype of an innovative system that eliminates the converter-dolly and thus the non-productive element that this component otherwise represents. Built around the requirement of moving two similar containers, each 7.15 m (23½ ft) in length and weighing 13 tonnes gross, the A-F system comprises two semi-trailers in standard format but is otherwise a complete deviation from the accepted practice.

The first trailer is the more important unit in the set and is equipped with a wide-spaced tandem-axle assembly fitted with single wheels and tyres. The axle assembly may be moved rearwards along the underside of the chassis and the rearmost axle, as well as being of the self-steer variety, also houses a fifth wheel.

For normal operation as a single semi-trailer, the unit looks and acts in a manner very similar to any other tandem-axle unit, although the single wheels and unusually wide spacing between the two axles do suggest that there is something special about it. But

for doubles work, the axles are moved rearwards so that the back axle acts as the converter-dolly for the second trailer, in this case a single-axle unit with twin wheels and tyres. Handling is improved by virtue of the steering facility of the first trailer's rear axle and the entire combination is designed to operate within West Germany's 18-m (59-ft) overall length limit and 38 tonnes gcw. It is a clever design, but complicated and expensive and, perhaps most importantly, like the B-train, it lacks the complete interchangeability offered by the standard double configuration.

In the strictest sense of the term, doubles are not found behind the Iron Curtain. Twin-trailer combinations in the A-train configuration are occasionally found, however, these operating primarily in the larger port cities or wherever a good road network exists.

Heavy-duty but old-fashioned Kraz 257 tractors are sometimes the motive units for the Soviet twin-trailer rigs, although more recently the 'third generation' Kamaz or perhaps the Maz 6000 series tractors are more likely to undertake this task in view of the larger, more powerful engines installed in these marques. In all cases, the configuration is a 6 × 4 unit coupled to a tandem-axle semi-trailer which, in turn, is hooked up to a two- or three-axle drawbar trailer. Bulk-fuel tanks and dropside trailers used for hauling both ISO and the smaller Soviet-built wooden crates are the only types thought to make up the Soviet A-trains, although some reports suggest that other commodities are hauled by this method.

Although the trains may be more efficient in terms of reducing manpower and motive effort, the speed at which they operate is hardly likely to improve overall efficiency. Twin-trailer combinations operating in Leningrad have been clocked at a sloth-like 15 mph (24 km/h) and, even at this speed, one outfit was seen with two flat tyres, one of which had completely shredded. In view of the low-axle weights generally allowed within the USSR, it seems unlikely that gross weights in excess of 48 tonnes would be feasible, even with a seven- or eight-axle rig. By way of comparison, a Maz 6422 truck or tractor coupled to a three-axle trailer (or semi) is more effective, grossing 42 tonnes but not being restricted by a very low maximum speed. However, this measurement is based on the

Western idea that speed of delivery is important, a factor not considered by the Soviets.

If nothing else, the Soviet twin-trailer combinations, however unusual, do indicate that the Soviets are at least starting to get to grips with the basic premise that, where conditions permit, it is not a bad idea to haul two, or even more, trailers in the overall interests of productivity. The problems would not appear to be related to space, since the main routes are built to motorway standard and large cities have exceptionally wide and spacious streets. More of a consideration perhaps is the availability of motive power suitable for hauling twin-trailer rigs, or even a shortage of qualified drivers. Whatever the reason, the idea of hauling two trailers has been adopted and it remains to be seen how quickly the concept will catch on.

Unfortunately, the semi-plus-pup outfits operating in the USSR also present a startling contrast with those combinations used elsewhere in the world. There is not much similarity, for example, between an ancient Kraz 257 hauling dirty and decrepit tankers around Leningrad and an exquisitely chromed

R aw salt is loaded aboard a huge Kenworth train by a massive conveyor. Corrosion of the sheet metal is a prime consideration so many aluminium components are included in the specification.

Marmon coupled to twin stainless-steel tanks trucking on through Michigan at an incredible all-up gross of 154,000 lbs (70 tonnes!). The trucks used on doubles work there may be an exception to the doubles rule but, in terms of appearance, payload and power, Michigan Trains present a picture that, once witnessed, is never forgotten.

The massive twin-trailer rigs operated in Michigan appear, at first glance to be very different from other 'doubles', simply because of the eleven rows of axles necessary to obtain the maximum gross weight. But there are other, less obvious, differences and the most important undoubtedly concerns the hook-up between the first and second trailers on dump-trailers.

Unlike almost all other doubles, the second trailer in a Michigan train dump-rig is a five-axle unit having the front two axles located on a ball race and not on the more customary divider dolly. The main reason for this layout is that it eliminates the need to wind down landing gear when the rearmost trailer is un-hooked during the tipping process. That is not to say that the method is perfect. Uncoupling the rearmost trailer once it has been unloaded involves uncoupling air, electrical and hydraulic lines as well as removing the twin safety chains and the giant pin. Once the lead trailer has been emptied, the uncoupling procedure has to be reversed, but not until the hook and eye have been successfully realigned. It is not a simple task to reverse one semi-trailer to a point where the divider dolly behind it picks up the kingpin of a second semi, but at least guide ramps allow for a little devi-ation. With a 'pin-and-eye' arrangement, no such latitude exists. The hook-up is either right in or right out, so a great deal of expertise is called for. That hav-ing been said, regular drivers of the huge trains go through a series of dumping operations as many as ten times per day and pick up the second trailer with a casual indifference that altogether disguises the enormous skill involved.

Autocar tractors are generally used by dump operators in Michigan, although International Pay-star 5000s and Mack DM 800s are also popular. Engines with at least 380 hp are required in order to meet minimum power-to-weight legislation and specs for both units and trailers are heavy duty, Michigan vehicles having a tendency to accept overloads as part of the everyday routine. In recent years, the trend away from big tube-type tyres has been followed by a rapid acceptance of tubeless low profiles and there can be little doubt that this has contributed towards longer tyre life and improved handling of the trains themselves. Low profiles are of course of particular value to tank-truck operators in Michigan since legis-lation restricting the overall height of such rigs was introduced in the interests of safety.

Glossary of Terms

'Double' *or 'double bottom'*   A rig comprising a trac-tor unit, a semi-trailer, a converter-dolly and a second semi-trailer.

West coast *double*   Generally a short-wheelbase cabover tractor with two trailers coupled as described above, used in the western USA.

Triple *or triple bottom*   Three semi-trailers, generally restricted to 26 ft or 27 ft in length, hauled behind a tractor unit and coupled together as in a doubles rig.

Eastern *double*   Twin trailers up to 45 ft in length hauled behind a three-axle tractor unit on specified routes in the eastern half of the USA.

Semi-plus-pup   Tractor unit coupled to a semi-trailer which in turn is hooked up to a generally shorter full or drawbar-style trailer. This combination sometimes described in Canada as an A-train.

B-train   Twin-trailer rig, designed initially in Canada, where a tractor unit is coupled to a specially designed semi-trailer which has its own fifth wheel assembly mounted at the rear end. A second semi-trailer can be coupled to the first using this fifth wheel.

Interlink   South African term used to describe the B-train hook-up.

Road Train   Any type of multi-trailer rig or, more specifically, a truck (as opposed to a tractive unit) hauling any number of full trailers or semi-trailers via dolly converters.

Michigan Train   Combinations of truck-trailers or twin-trailers rolling on eleven axles in Michigan. Also known as Great Lakes Specials. Multi-axle semi-trailers used to haul coils of steel are known as 'Cen-tipede' trailers and the rig is not a genuine Michigan train.

Mixed Doubles   A twin-trailer rig made up of, say, a box trailer and a tank trailer.

DROM BOXES

The origins of the word 'dromedary' when applied to the trucking industry are a little obscure, but it seems reasonable to suppose that there is some connection with the ability of both the camel and the tractor unit to carry something on their backs.

Certainly drom-equipped tractors are not common, being confined almost entirely to North America, where they have been used for over 30 years, but interesting examples do crop up elsewhere and, at different times, Scandinavian countries, New Zealand, Australia and even the UK have witnessed their own versions. Today they are still found in Canada, the USA, Sweden and New Zealand, but recent examples in other areas are rather less in evidence.

Mounted ahead of the fifth wheel coupling, the 'drom' (which may be a box or a tank) serves a variety of functions. Naturally it is most frequently used to accommodate additional freight but, in the USA, these outwardly uninspiring constructions are often used by husband-and-wife driver teams as living

Although Volvo and Scania dominate the Swedish truck market, a few Ford Transcontinental tractors were sold there. Among the more interesting examples is this lovely 5235 6 × 2 dromedary rig.

A real puzzle is this unusual dromedary-double operated by Heatons Transport in New Zealand. Crusader tractor features a huge drom box and is coupled to a van semi-trailer and dropside pup.

quarters. All the comforts of home are provided and many droms boast not only the now fairly common-place microwave oven and TV but also a self-contained shower, refrigerator and even a washing machine.

Cab comforts have come a long way in recent years and top-of-the-range versions, such as Kenworth's Aerodyne or Volvo's Globetrotter provide a level of comfort and convenience not even dreamed of 25 years ago. Yet despite these advances, even the biggest truck cab can become confined and cluttered after a long, uninterrupted spell on the road and long-haul drivers will tell you there is no substitute for being able to climb down from behind the wheel and straight into your own private hotel. True, a drom may not be the five-star Hilton, but it is always nearby and never overbooked! Owner-operators contracted to the big American household movers, such as May-flower, Allied or North American, can be away from home for months at a time and to these people a drom is both a necessity and a big money-saver.

B ecause of liberal size and weight laws in Sweden, even tractor-trailer combinations can be 24 m (79 ft) in overall length. Such lengths are generally impractical, however, but one solution is to use a drom box on a long-wheelbase tractor and to haul a 40-ft trailer. Magnusson's superb 8 × 2 Volvo F12 (converted from a 6 × 2) is probably the biggest tractor in Europe, and is certainly far larger than the Danish rig 'Mr Brandit', which so often claims this distinction.

Some droms were designed and built with a more specific purpose in mind, an example being a highly sophisticated box which slides to and fro along the chassis rails of its host vehicle, a 9670 cabover International tractor in order to make loading and unloading simpler. The complete rig, comprising a long-

wheelbase drom tractor and semi-trailer, is used exclusively for the transportation of babies' nappies (or diapers in American parlance) and because this load posed problems of volume as opposed to weight, the owner, Black's Transport, specified a rig offering the maximum load area.

By using a 15 ft (4.6 m) long drom box and a 46 ft (14 m) Roussy Industries semi-trailer, a load space length totalling 61 ft (18.6 m) was possible within the legal overall maximum of 68 ft 10 in (21 m). This offered vital additional load space over the more conventional method of using two semi-trailers but did incur a few complications along the way. Most obvious was the tremendous length of the tractor itself and its poor turning circle. But despite the use of oversize tyres on

the 16,500-lb (7.5-tonnes) capacity front axle, the steering linkage was modified sufficiently to allow a better wheel cut. The end result was a turning circle not much worse than that of a far shorter tractor unit.

Sweden's approach to drom boxes is at variance with that of North America for the reason, once again, of legislation. Maximum weights and overall lengths are by far the most generous in Europe but, in complete contrast to the USA, legislation favours the use of truck-trailer combinations and tractor-trailers are found in small numbers only. Put simply, in order to take full advantage of the 51.4-tonne gtw and 24 m (78¾ ft) length limit, a three-axle truck pulling a three- or four-axle full trailer is required. A tractor/semi-trailer combination cannot hope to meet

Long-wheelbased Kenworth K-100 cabover sleeper equipped with large drom box provides living accommodation for the husband-and-wife removal team.

Since the Surface Transportation Assistance Act was introduced in the USA, tractor units have increased in size. Many now feature expensive drom-box living accommodation such as this $40,000 Liv-Lab mounted on the already extravagantly finished Peterbilt 362 unit. An unusual feature is the exhaust routed underneath the fuel tank.

A rarity in the UK, this Atkinson twin-steer unit carried a salt silo in front of the fifth wheel coupling and a further pair of silos were mounted on the tandem-axle semi-trailer.

the axle-loading requirements if high gross weights are to be hauled and yet there are obviously 12.2 m (40 ft) trailers employed on international traffic and, as these inevitably end up in Sweden at some stage, someone has to move them.

The answer here is to use a drom-equipped tractor, since this can be of any length and, as such, can accommodate a fairly hefty box behind the cab. Most Swedish droms are installed on long-wheelbase Volvo or Scania three-axle units, and, although there is no legal restriction on the size of these boxes, practical limitations imposed by turning circles and general handling generally mean that the droms are about 8 ft to 12 ft (2.4 to 3.7 m) in length. One Swedish operator, bent on obtaining the maximum possible payload while reducing the possibility of a front-axle overload, has modified his Volvo F12 long-wheelbase 6 × 2 tractor to an 8 × 2 by adding a second steering axle. Installed by Møller of Copenhagen in Denmark, the air-suspended second-steer axle has not only ensured that the Volvo will never be overloaded but has also produced one of the most interesting and spectacular units currently operating in Sweden!

Swedish manufacturers, Volvo and Scania, are smugly confident about sales in their own country and, when asked about market share, will state that each has 50% and the rest they leave to the imports!

While this is not strictly true, in the heavy sector these figures are not far from the truth and few importers have made any appreciable penetration into

the Swedish market. One of the reasons is the remark-ably stringent ruling covering cab safety and this alone has effectively prevented most European manu-facturers from selling any of their products. An excep-tion was the Ford TransContinental and sixty-seven of these tall, handsome vehicles found their way into the hands of Swedish operators in a decade. A few were converted from 4 × 2 units to 6 × 2s and stretched in the process to allow the installation of a drom box. Designated 5235, the big Fords used Cum-mins 350s for power and were rated at 52-tonnes gtw in order to comply with Swedish operating require-ments. When coupled to a tri-axle European-style semi-trailer, these long-wheelbase units with large-capacity fuel tanks located alongside the chassis frame rails made a spectacular sight, especially when decorated with chrome and aluminium extras and extravagant paintwork.

Built to take full advantage of the 62-tonne gtw for doubles permitted in Canada's western province of British Columbia and, at the same time, to be versatile enough to carry the maximum payload allowed for

Drom boxes have different functions and this unit is employed in order to gain the maximum volume. In order to speed up loading and unloading, the entire drom box slides rearwards to the end of the frame. A recess in the centre allows passage over the fifth wheel. Tractor is a 9670 International.

single trailers when on city deliveries, Inland Fuel's dromedary-tractor-B-train was the first of its kind.

Inland's requirements were not easy to satisfy but the end product resulting from months of research by operator and manufacturer was startling. Most inter-esting was the 900-Imperial-gallon (4,090-litre) drom tank located on the long-wheelbase Freightliner tractor. This not only gave extra capacity when used with the two semi-trailers but also added valuable payload when coupled to the 8,600-Imperial-gallon (39,095-litre) tri-axle semi-trailer which formed the rear part of the B-train rig. This 6-axle tractor-trailer offering a total of 9,500 Imperial gallons (43,187 litres) could then operate at the maximum permitted weight of 45.5 tonnes for city work where single-trailer rigs only were allowed.

Australian 8 × 4 Atkinson with 'Skippy' glass-fibre cab features a dromedary milk tank ahead of the fifth wheel. This style of Atkinson has been replaced by the later International-inspired unit but was very popular with Australian operators.

Specifications for the Inland Freightliner included a Detroit Diesel 8V92TA rated at 440 hp, Fuller RT12515 and Eaton 20-tonne rear axles. Neway air suspension was used throughout in the interests of axle loadings.

Other examples of drom units include an 8 × 4 Atkinson tractor equipped with a large capacity tank and, perhaps more exotic, a four-axle Scammell Crusader which featured a large freight box ahead of the fifth wheel.

These units, used in Australia and New Zealand respectively, accentuate the very different configurations found in use overseas on vehicles whose origins are well known to British operators.

Another type of drom tractor has a load space behind the cab and ahead of the fifth wheel which can be used to carry a few pallets or perhaps one single coil of steel. Reasons behind this unusual layout are largely legislative and concern overall lengths and axle loadings.

INDEX

Addendum
During recent months, twin-trailer 'doubles' combinations have been introduced in France and B-train rigs have started to appear in different areas of Australia where their performance is being closely monitored.